D1462962

2 66
14

STAN MUSIAL: BASEBALL'S DURABLE "MAN"

"I think I always had a bat and ball in my hands," Stan Musial once told a reporter years after he had become a great hitter and equally great sports attraction. This is the story of Stan's life both as a great hitter with numerous baseball records to his credit and as a man. Beginning with his early life in Donora, Pennsylvania, and continuing through the 1962 season in which Stan's final average was third highest in the National League, the author speculates on how many years Stan can keep playing for the St. Louis Cardinals. This portrait of Stan Musial is made more vivid with quotes from Stan's friends and family.

STAN MUSIAL:

BASEBALL'S DURABLE "MAN"

by Ray Robinson

G. P. PUTNAM'S SONS

New York

CONTENTS

To Phyllis,
my home-grown .400 hitter

STAN MUSIAL:

Baseball's Durable "Man"

CHAPTER ONE

THE BOY FROM DONORA

Donora, Pennsylvania, on the banks of the sluggish Monongahela River, is a bleak mill town of some 15,000 hard-working souls. The grass, stained by perennial smog, is never very green. And the skies are often blacker than the inside of an umpire's pockets. Donora is 25 miles from Pittsburgh, so most of the kids in town grow up rooting for the Pittsburgh Pirates.

But since 1941, when Stanley Frank Musial of Donora played his first game in the uniform of the St. Louis Cardinals, the youngsters of the town, as well as their dads, uncles, and mothers, have made Stan their Number One hero.

Donora may have discovered Stan Musial before the rest of America. But for years it has had to share him with literally millions of other Americans, who happen to be Musial fans.

The story you are about to read is an appreciation of a true American sports hero.

*　*　*

The August sun, fiercely dazzling but welcome, made the lanky young man, not quite fifteen years old, squint as he peered studiously at the batter 60 feet away. He was left-handed and, in the tradition of southpaws, already wild enough to force the respect and undivided attention of the batter.

In less than six full innings of pitching he had struck out 12 batters. Now he had two strikes on the batter, with two out in the ninth inning. One more good strike — he was certain he had that one up his left sleeve — and he would be the winning pitcher against the vaunted sluggers of the Monessen, Pennsylvania, club.

"Ya got him, Stashu," yelled the squatting catcher, "give it to me here!"

A suspicion of a grin crossed the pitcher's face. Carefully he concealed the ball in his glove. Then his spikes took a firm grip on the hard little anthill at Palmer Park, the right leg shot up, then the left arm reared back, and the ball hummed and blurred as it buried itself in the big catcher's mitt.

"Strike three, you're out," the umpire bellowed, without a moment's uncertainty.

An hour before, the pitcher had been the bat boy for Manager Joe Barbao's zinc works' semipro team. In a moment of rare inspiration Manager Barbao had called upon the lad to pitch. And now he had done a man's job, striking out 13 batters and winning the ball game.

"You looked just like Lefty Grove out there just now, Stan," said Joe. "You never showed me that much when we practiced back of the house."

"I've been holding out on you," the team's new star pitcher laughed.

Stan Musial had been playing baseball since he was scarcely eight years old.

"I think I always had a bat and ball in my hands," he once told a reporter many years later, when he had become, not the greatest pitcher of his time, but the greatest hitter.

First he played catch in back of his house on Marelda Street. The house, like most of those in Donora, was unpretentious and cramped. It was built in 1903, and had four rooms for Stan's four sisters, one brother and himself. But Mrs. Musial, who worked as a house-keeper for other folks in town, kept the place spotless.

"When I could make a little time for it," Stan Musial's mother recalls, "I used to play ball with him in the yard. But I was mostly busy working. Mr. Musial never had an easy time of it. There wasn't much money."

Lukasz Musial, Stan's father, was an immigrant from

11

Poland, like so many others who had settled in Donora to work in its mills.

Life in the old country and here, in the new country of hope and liberty and opportunity, had never been easy for Lukasz Musial. When he worked, lifting heavy bundles of wire at the American Steel and Wire Company, which was to Donora what the Ford plant is to Detroit, he worked hard. Sometimes after work, to relax his tired muscles and his strained back, he drank too much — more than was good for him.

Mary Lancos, his wife, was the daughter of a Czech miner. She was in her teens when she met Lukasz for the first time. Money was short in the Lancos home, too, and Mary, a woman of determination and pride, went to work in a zinc factory.

When Mary married Lukasz Musial, they settled in the little house on Marelda Street. Four girls were born into the household before Stan arrived on November 21, 1920. After Stan there was still another boy.

Though he was somewhat frail-looking as a youngster, Stan took to his dad's favorite sport of tumbling. The two of them journeyed, hand in hand, to the Polish National Alliance each week. And Lukasz was happy about Stan's tumbling, for this was, he thought, the kind of activity that helped to build a child into a virile man with muscles and agility.

However, the rising generation of immigrant offspring in Donora began to show a sharp preference for

12

the sports that were more typical of America. So Stan started to play basketball, at which he was quite good, and baseball, which also seemed to come to him naturally. The boy's devotion to basketball did not disturb Lukasz as much as the baseball playing did.

"Maybe he can get a scholarship to college with the basketball," said Lukasz to Mary one evening, as they sat in the tiny dining room of their house pondering their boy's future.

As far as the Musials were concerned, there wasn't the slightest doubt that their growing son was destined to attend one of those fine American universities, where a man learned to do something besides working in the mills. The hard, unremitting daily grind that they, as poor immigrants, were enduring in a strange land would be worth it if their boy could get an education.

If basketball, at which Stan was now excelling in Donora High School, could help to put him in college, then perhaps it wasn't a waste of time. But baseball, thought Lukasz, was a total waste. How could anyone spend so much time at it?

"It is important that you study hard," Lukasz lectured his son, "so some day you can go to college."

Stan was an obedient son. He was not rebellious or stubborn and he liked his teachers and his books.

But that didn't mean that when Joe Barbao, who was a neighbor and a semipro pitcher, came by to have a catch with Stan or to take him out to Palmer Park as his team's bat boy, Stan turned him down. To the contrary, for Stan loved baseball already. He loved the feel of the ball in his hand, the smell of the ragged glove that he kept in a safe place in his drawer. And he had heard of the great ballplayers in Pittsburgh, like the agile third baseman Pie Traynor and the two Waner brothers, Paul and Loyd, who had the strange nicknames of Big Poison and Little Poison.

Stan liked football, too. But here Lukasz definitely put his foot down.

"A boy can waste so much time playing these sports. When can he study?" Lukasz appealed to Mary. It did not occur to Lukasz, an unsophisticated man, that football, rather than basketball, might be a much surer path to college for Stan. For there were many colleges then, as there are now, that awarded scholarships to boys who could kick and pass a football with skill.

When he was seventeen years old Stan led the Donora High School basketball team to an undefeated season. At one point during the year he came down with a bad case of pneumonia. Jim Russell, his coach, valued the boy's abilities so much that Stan stayed at the Russell home for almost a month, where Mrs. Russell helped to nurse him back to health.

Although Stan was never an A student, he worked hard at his studies and had great respect for his teachers and coaches.

"He never gave anyone any trouble," recalls Jim

Russell, whose good name has been associated with Donora High's athletic teams for over three decades.

Andrew S. Sukel, who was the principal of Donora High School when Stan was a pupil there (today Sukel is the superintendent of Donora's public schools), has fond memories of the early years that Stan spent in his school.

"Stan was the kind of boy that he is now as a man," says Sukel, with a good deal of feeling. "What he has done as a gentleman and as a sportsman is exactly the way he was at school. He always handled himself properly and instinctively said and did the right thing. He was quiet and polite. The fact he came from a very poor family only served to increase the respect people had for him."

Even today, when he is nationally famous and wealthy, Stan refuses to forget the old home town and the humble beginnings that sent him on his way. For the first few years after he left the grimy, gritty Donora streets to launch his big league career with the Cardinals, Musial never failed to return to his birthplace in the off-season. He would work in his father-in-law's grocery store and visit with his old friends.

"He was a familiar sight around town," says Sukel. "He loved to associate a lot with the older men — his teachers and coaches — and talk about the old days.

"Once I remember he came over to the high school with a good buddy of his — a St. Louis sportswriter —

15

to take a look at a transcript of his school academic record. He looked at it for a long while, carefully and with a serious face. Then he said to me, 'I could have done better than this, don't you think?'

"Many times during the off-season Stan would come over to our high school gym to work out on the basketball court. He liked to keep in good trim for the spring training period — and I guess he often arrived in Florida in as good shape as any ballplayer you can think of.

"But he never once stepped on that school basketball court without asking my permission first. He'd drop by my office and say: 'Mr. Sukel, can I use the gym today?'

"One day I said to him, 'Stan, from now on you don't have to bother asking me. For goodness sakes, just come up here and play. We're delighted and honored to have you.'

"But don't you think he kept right on asking my permission every time he came by to use the court? That's the kind of man Stan Musial is. He's a classic example for the youngsters of America to follow."

All of Stan's friends from Donora — and he has multitudes of them — regard him with genuine affection, mainly because they know him as a person who has never changed and has never failed to do kind things.

"He's never forgotten a single friend," insists Frank A. Pizzica, who runs a local semipro basketball team in Donora and also owns a garage in which Stan has spent many a happy hour just shooting the breeze.

"I've never heard a derogatory remark about Stan, either as a youngster or since he became the greatest hitter of all," says Pizzica. "And he deserves that kind of reputation. He's generous to his home town, his sisters and brother, and his church. He's built his mother a beautiful home on the outskirts of Donora. At Christmastime there isn't a single old buddy, and that especially includes his former teachers, who aren't remembered with a card.

"Some years ago I visited Stan in St. Louis for the All-Star Game. Our train pulled into town a little before five o'clock in the morning. But don't you think that Stan, with a big smile on his mug, was waiting there at the station — even at that hour! That's the kind of a fellow he is. Nobody has ever written about a nicer fellow!"

If there seems to be a quality of unreality, of Frank Merriwell fiction about this man, if his character and personality and behavior seem too good, too exemplary, if he has been able to combine his skills with tact and taste, that *is* the way he is, and has always been.

No press agents have been ushered into service to win Stan Musial increased homage or affection. None has been necessary. His deeds, thoughts and actions, on the field and off the field, have won him his reputation.

Musial owns so many diverse major league marks

17

that some pundits have insisted he boasts more records than a disc jockey. In Stan's extraordinary case, that is almost beside the point. What is important, as Bob Burnes, a St. Louis sportswriter, has stated it, is that Stan "will go down in baseball history as the most beloved, the most honored, the most admired, the most complete player the game has ever known."

There have been the Ruths for sheer, unadulterated batting power. There have been the Cobbs for dash, élan and anger. There have been the Williamses for skill, discipline and compulsive desire. There have been the Gehrigs for durability. There have been the Mayses for exuberance and sheer instinct.

But there is only one steady-eyed Stan Musial.

Where will baseball ever find another to equal his consistent brilliance?

CHAPTER TWO

BIRTH OF A REDBIRD

In the depression days of the 1930s, when Americans listened eagerly to Franklin D. Roosevelt's "fireside chats," while Europeans shrank from the strident cadence of the Nazi jackboots, Stan Musial took the first important steps of his budding career.

While he was the kind of youngster who helped out around the house when he could, Stan always managed to find time to play ball. More often than not he'd be out at Palmer Park, where he'd throw and hit baseballs until he was almost exhausted.

When he was in his teens he tagged a ball one day that went well over 400 feet. It is one of those legendary drives that everyone who grew up in Stan's home town claims he saw. Bobby Thomson's home run against the

Brooklyn Dodgers at the Polo Grounds in 1951, to win a pennant and a playoff for the Giants, also claims an increasingly large audience every year.

Lil Labash, whose dad owned a grocery store in Donora, was one of the earliest to discover the talents of Stan Musial. One day when Lil, who was only fourteen at the time, was taken to Palmer Park to watch a ball game between men in their twenties and thirties, she was surprised to see a "skinny Polish kid" pitching. Stan, who was just fourteen, could already do everything as well or better than his fellow players and Lil was quick to notice it.

Stan pitched with confidence and poise, for a lad of such a tender age, and Lil was deeply impressed. "I thought he was such an amazing boy!" Lil says, recalling with warmth the first glimpse of the youngster she was eventually to marry.

Shortly after Lil's first view of Stan on a pitcher's mound, the two started to date. She attended most of the basketball games that Stan played in, went skating with him and walking with him. If there was a dream in Stan's mind of better things for his family and for himself, Lil did not know of it, for Stan was a quiet young man who was not always able to articulate his feelings and reduce them into a few words.

Many times Stan was late for dates with Lil. But he had an excellent excuse. The ball park was directly on the road to Lil's house and he never missed an opportunity to watch a ball game in progress. This is a habit that as a man and a major-leaguer he has never outgrown. In St. Louis Hills, where he has lived for many years, it is a rare day when he doesn't stop his car next to the park to watch the youngsters play.

Stan worked after school to help his dad meet expenses. With the money he earned at various jobs he bought most of his own clothes.

"He really didn't have much clothes," Lil says, "but he was always neat as a pin."

Lil and Stan often would meet in her dad's grocery store. When Stan pitched in to help in the store his reward was a sandwich and a bottle of milk. To this day Lil chides Stan about their early relationship.

"You know why you went out with me?" asks Lil. "Only because my father owned that grocery store and fed you so well."

Lil and Stan were inseparable for almost five years. So nobody in Donora was the least bit surprised when Stan and Lil were married on November 21, 1939, a day that also happened to be Stan's nineteenth birthday.

By that time Stan had already embarked on the baseball career that was to make him famous. But the two years before Stan married, and before he made his life commitment to baseball, were difficult ones in the Musial household.

Dr. Michael Duda, who was Stan's baseball coach at Donora High School, was well aware of the feelings

21

that Lukasz Musial had about baseball as a profession for his son.

"Stan wanted to be a ballplayer from the start," says Dr. Duda. "He stuck to it, too, in the face of some pretty keen obstacles at home."

The more the major league scouts beat a path to the Musial door, the more Lukasz Musial resented what his son was about to do with his life. Lukasz had a simple but understandable point of view about the matter. Having worked hard all of his life at manual tasks and physical jobs which required limited skills, he was determined that his boy should go to college, possibly the University of Pittsburgh, which he had heard about.

"At college you can play basketball," said Lukasz. "But this baseball is nothing more than a waste of time."

"But that's what I want to do more than anything else in the world," Stan would plead.

Rather than disturb his father endlessly on the subject, Stan sought advice from others. He spoke to Joe Barbao who, of course, couldn't conceive of Stan doing anything else but play baseball. Stan's friends at school, including Mr. Sukel and Dr. Duda and Mr. Russell, did not like to oppose Stan's father. But they all shared the feeling that Stan should do what his heart was set on doing. Though Stan respected his father and knew the depth of his feelings against baseball, and for a college education, he also respected the opinions of the people at school, who knew him well enough not to mislead him.

If Stan had had his own way, of course, he would have signed on immediately with his favorites, the Pittsburgh Pirates. Joe Barbao continually tried to persuade the Pittsburgh team to sign his young protégé. But the Pirates were not quite as convinced as another major league club, the St. Louis Cardinals, that the skinny young southpaw was worth signing up. However, Stan did get to work out with the Pirates and it is recorded history that the Pittsburgh team did make some move to sign the boy from Donora.

That Stan got away from the Pirates is attributable more perhaps to Stan's desire to get a few miles away from home than to an error of judgment by the front office of the Pirates.

It seems the Pirates had intentions to send the lad to a farm team that was situated near Donora. Stan, on the other hand, with a bit of the wanderlust in his heart, had visions of great cities and hamlets that he might see for the first time by virtue of his promising baseball skill.

The first time that the Cards, through their scout Andy French, then manager of the Monessen Club in the Pennsylvania State Association, approached Stan to sign a contract, Lukasz Musial would have none of it.

"I won't let my boy sign any contract to play base-

23

ball," said Mr. Musial. And the tone of his voice was harsh and final.

However, the Cards, fresh from their triumphs with the rambunctious and renowned Gashouse Gang, and with the smoothest functioning farm system in baseball, would not take no for an answer. They insisted that Andy French keep prodding the boy with a fountain pen full of ink.

One day, when French visited the Musial house to discuss the situation again with the Musials, Andy seemed to be making headway with his cajolery.

But then Lukasz Musial, who still had the shining vision of his boy attending one of America's fine universities and could see him as a lawyer or a doctor or an engineer, balked again.

"I will not be talked into it," said Lukasz stubbornly.

French shrugged his shoulders.

"I think you are passing up an excellent opportunity for your boy," said Andy, "but if that's the way you feel I guess I'll leave. There's no sense wasting any more of my time or yours."

Stan Musial, seventeen, an unspoiled, thoughtful, considerate youth, could see his dreams evaporating into thin air. He respected his elders too much to raise his voice in argument and he was not the type to stomp out of the room in a rage at his father's intransigence.

But, as he heard his father's words, tears welled up in his eyes. Concerned that French might catch him crying, Stan blew his nose into his handkerchief. If it was any solace to Stan, Andy French felt like crying at that moment, too.

Then a strange thing happened.

Lukasz Musial, seeing his son's tears, seemed to realize for the first time how much playing baseball meant to his boy. The strategic moment had arrived for some persuasive oratory. Andy French had already failed in this department. It now remained for Mary Musial, Stan's secret weapon, to supply the ammunition to change her husband's mind.

"Lukasz," began Mary Musial, "you have always told me this is a free country and that is why you love it so much. Isn't your boy free to do what his heart desires? Must he go to college against his wishes? I think he should have his chance to play baseball, if that is really what he wants."

Lukasz turned to look at Stan. Tears formed tiny rivulets on the youngster's cheeks. Then he motioned to Andy French.

"Do you have the contract?" he said, almost in a whisper. It was like asking Andy if he liked to breathe.

Without another word Andy produced the contract from his inside pocket.

Lukasz, not a learned man, let his eyes rest on the contract for a moment.

"What will you pay my boy?" he asked.

"He will receive $65 a month for five months," said French.

"Where do I sign?"

French spread the contract on the living room table. "Here," he pointed.

There wasn't a sound in the room, except the scratching of his pen, as Lukasz carefully inscribed his name on a contract that would make his son a baseball player in the St. Louis Cardinals' organization.

CHAPTER THREE

THE HOUSE IN HOUSTON

Some players spend a lifetime in the uniform of a single ball club. It was that way with little Mel Ott of the New York Giants, Lou Gehrig of the New York Yankees, Ted Williams of the Boston Red Sox and Joltin' Joe DiMaggio of the New York Yankees.

It is that way, too, with Stan Musial of the Cardinals. He will always be a hero in St. Louis. It is impossible, after all of these years, to imagine him ever playing for another baseball team.

Yet Stan Musial almost missed being a Cardinal!

Not long after Lukasz Musial reluctantly put his signature on his underage son's first baseball contract, Judge Kenesaw Mountain Landis, the stern commissioner of baseball, who had contributed so much to

Stan Musial as he looked in 1941, his first season with the Cardinals after three years in the Redbirds' farm system.

the rehabilitation of the game's reputation in the 1920s, issued a ruling from his high office. He said that some 91 Cardinal farm hands, including Stan Musial, had not been signed properly by the Cards. The ruling made all of these players free agents. It put them in a position to sign again with any team they wanted.

Stan Musial could then have become a Pirate, or a Dodger or a Giant — or, if he wanted — a Cardinal again.

Eddie Dyer, who was then the supervisor of the far-flung St. Louis farm system (later he managed the Cards), immediately prevailed upon the young player to sign again with the Cards. Dyer was convinced the boy had the makings of a great star and he was determined not to let him get away to another club where in future years he would return to haunt the Cards.

Stan was not quite certain what to do. But he trusted Eddie Dyer's good judgment, despite the fact Dyer represented a particular point of view.

"I know you want to help me with this problem," Stan said to Dyer one day. "If I were your kid brother what would you advise me to do about this?"

Dyer, a man with a generous-sized nose and a soft Southern accent, looked straight into Stan's eyes.

"Son, I'd sign with the Cardinals," said Dyer.

So, for the second time in his life, Stan signed with the Cardinals. It became, then, Stan and the Redbirds, an alliance as natural to baseball fans as pitcher is to catcher.

But first, of course, Stan Musial, like so many other eager apprentice ballplayers, had to prove himself in the minors. Few great players have been able to make the stiff leap from the sandlot or the high school diamond directly to the majors. Stan was no exception.

The first minor league baseball assignment for Stan was with the Class D Williamson team in the Mountain States League. Williamson, only a tiny town in West Virginia, was Stan's first great adventure away from home and, though he was making only $65 a month, he fancied himself the luckiest young man in the world.

Those who came in contact with him at Williamson were impressed with him more as a youngster of sterling character than as a pitcher. "He is truly a fine boy, with good habits," said Wid Matthews, who roamed all over the Cardinal farm system for Branch Rickey, the bushy-browed genius who ran the organization.

Stan's personal conduct and habits were impeccable, as always. But his performance on the mound supported the old theory that left-handers are born to be wild men and to make their penmanship teachers suffer.

In his first season, 1938, as a pitcher for Williamson, Stan won six games and lost six games. But he walked 80 batters in 110 innings. His bat was relatively silent, too, for he hit only a single homer. The overall record scarcely marked him as a coming titan of the game.

felt he hadn't made a mistake to embark on a baseball career, despite his dad's desires. He lived simply, eating cheese sandwiches with plenty of mustard, and hot dogs and hamburgers. Every now and then he'd treat himself to a steak. But that was a rarity, for part of his small salary was sent to his family each month to help out at home.

At the close of the 1938 season Stan came home and went to work in the Labash grocery store. If all else failed, naturally, he could always settle down behind the counter. But Stan had no notion that he wouldn't make it.

Stan did a good deal better for Williamson in 1939. He won nine games and lost only two. But the discouraging part was that he got into only 13 games as a pitcher. On the other hand, when the Williamson manager felt he was a little short on hitting talent he began to call on Stan for pinch-hitting chores. In this role Stan was able to amass a .352 batting average, which was an accurate harbinger of things to come.

After Stan's marriage in the off-season of 1939, he was shifted to Daytona Beach, Florida, of the Class D Florida State League. It was there that he met and worked under a unique baseball man, who was to become one of the prime influences of his career.

Little Dickie Kerr was that man. When Stan first met him he was the manager of the Daytona Beach ball

But Stan liked what he was doing. In his heart he

club. Stan could find no better man after whom to pattern himself. Kerr had been a stouthearted left-handed pitcher, who worked valiantly but against great odds to win the 1919 World Series for the Chicago White Sox against the Cincinnati Reds. The great odds were that more than a handful of his teammates — eight, to be exact — had refused to give their best efforts in that infamous series, which is better known in baseball history as the Black Sox Scandal. Dickie managed, despite the plotting of his fellow players, to win two games in that series. Thus, he rates consideration as one of the legitimate heroes of big league history.

This was the man who, having survived his own darkest moment, came to the aid of Stan Musial when that eager young man appeared to be on the verge of giving up baseball and returning to the smog of Donora.

Ironically, Stan was having a fine year when an incident occurred that almost caused him to lose faith in himself and his future. If it hadn't been for the thoughtful and patient influence of Dickie Kerr, Stan might have put his glove in mothballs for all time.

As a pitcher for Kerr's Daytona Beach team in 1940, Stan had a splendid season. He won 18 games and lost only five. His control, which was noticeably lacking in his first two seasons at Williamson, seemed substantially improved and Kerr used him in regular rotation.

But Dickie had noticed something else about this quiet nineteen-year-old. He discovered that he was a hitting pitcher. When Stan was in the lineup as a pitcher more often than not he'd send line drives whistling to all corners of the field when he'd get his turn at bat.

"He was too good to be kept on the bench between pitching starts," remembers Kerr. So the little pilot started to use Stan as an outfielder on the afternoons when he wasn't pitching. The innovation, which was quite helpful to a team that had only 15 players on the roster, ultimately made Stan's career.

But at first it almost destroyed him.

On the night of August 11, 1940, Stan was playing center field. Like Dickie Kerr, Stan has always been an all-out ballplayer. It was that way that long-ago night when a line drive came sizzling out to Stan's territory. Making a tumbling, stumbling effort to overhaul the ball, Stan made a spectacular shoestring catch. But he fell heavily on his left shoulder.

Stan knew something went in his shoulder as soon as he got to his feet. But he hated to admit that tumbling, which was the sport of his father, could be the cause of his ruination as a pitcher. So, although nursing secret doubts about his left arm, he took his regular turn as a pitcher. He won one start against the Sanford club, in a squeaker. But when he started a game against Orlando he was as ineffective as a Little Leaguer pitching against giants.

He knew then that he had to tell Dickie Kerr, in all

33

frankness, that he suspected his pitching days were numbered.

Stan felt he could talk to Kerr as he would to his own father, for Kerr had a genuine liking for him and enjoyed giving him advice.

Their relationship already was full of mutual respect and trust. There was the time, for instance, that Dickie Kerr discovered Stan in a hotel lobby at 7 A.M. one Sunday morning. For many players in those days this was an hour in which they would be returning to their hotels, after an evening of gallivanting and celebrating. Not knowing Stan too well at the time, Kerr looked at the boy with a suspicious eye.

"Where ya been?" asked the manager, scarcely expecting to hear anything resembling the truth.

"I'm just coming from Mass," answered Stan.

Kerr didn't have the slightest doubt that his young pitcher was telling the truth. Almost from that moment on his interest in Stan intensified. He was convinced baseball needed more youngsters like this brown-eyed youth, and he would do anything to help him.

Now Stan was coming to him for help — and counsel.

"I don't think I can pitch any more with my bad left shoulder," said Stan, resignedly. "And Lil is going to have a baby, so I think the wise thing for me to do is to quit and go back home and get a good paying job in the mills."

Even before he could blurt out his rebuttal, Kerr was shaking his head vigorously, from side to side, at Stan's defeatist proposal.

"You can't quit, Stan," he said. "You've got a future in this game as a hitter. If you ever get up to the big leagues they'll want you in there every day for your hitting. You'll stay in the lineup as an outfielder."

When Stan insisted that his career didn't seem very promising at this stage of the game, Kerr, who had a rare insight into the boy, suggested that Stan move in with him. He told Stan that he and his wife had just rented a larger house at Daytona Beach and it might make a nice spot for Lil to come home to after the baby was born.

The Musials accepted the invitation. Stan felt that Lil would be terribly lonely without any of her family around. This arrangement, due to Kerr's kindness, would give Lil the companionship she needed so badly at such a time in her life. It would also enable him to get along a bit better on the $100-a-month salary he was then earning with the ball club.

When the baby was born he was named Richard, after Dickie Kerr.

"I'll never forget the Kerrs and how wonderful they were to us," Stan has said. "They treated us just like their own children. I'll never be able to repay what they did for us."

Quietly, and without fanfare, some eighteen years

later, Stan Musial tried to repay Dickie Kerr, in his own way, for what Kerr had done for him in those crucial days of his budding career.

Kerr was sixty-five years old, and though he had led an honorable and hard-working life in the profession he loved best, baseball had never treated him as kindly as he had treated it. Back in the early twenties, after the Black Sox Scandal, he had stayed out of organized ball for three years after a contract dispute with the White Sox ownership. When he finally returned to active duty his talents had all but deserted him. Thus, he had experienced an abbreviated career, and never had had an opportunity to amass any savings.

Sensitive to Kerr's situation, and, by 1958, one of baseball's most affluent players, Stan made up his mind to help his counselor of the early years. When the St. Louis club was passing through Houston, Kerr's home town, during the spring training season of 1958, Stan stopped by to call on the Kerrs.

"You're having a birthday soon," said Stan, who knew Dickie was born in July, "and I'd like to give you a nice present — a house."

The Kerrs were overwhelmed. At first they would have no part of Stan's grandiose plan. But Stan had made up his mind that this was what he wanted for his dear friends.

"You pick out what you want," he insisted, "and I'll take care of it."

36

The house that the Kerrs selected was a $10,000 home in Houston. For a while after the Kerrs moved in there was no mention anyplace of the gratuity and that's exactly the way Stan wanted it.

But in time the Houston newspapers broke the story. When one New York columnist got wind of the deed he dubbed it unqualifiedly as the "human interest story of the year."

The most interesting reaction of all was the fact that one and all agreed that the gift was perfectly consistent with Stan's character. Not a soul even hinted that it was designed to get publicity for Musial. On the contrary, when Stan was besieged by reporters he flatly refused to talk further about the revelation.

The Kerrs, on the other hand, were in seventh heaven. They were perfectly happy to tell the entire world about the wonderful thing that Stan Musial had done for them.

"This is the luckiest thing that ever happened to us," the Kerrs exclaimed. "The Musials are truly wonderful people."

Stan's fellow players had known for years what a decent man he was, in every sense of the word. But now even those without any interest in batting averages and broken records were learning about the true dimensions of this superb athlete who had come from such humble beginnings.

There is a plaque that was presented to Stan by his

teammates several years ago. The inscription on it is a true measure of the man. It says this of Stan:

TO STANLEY FRANK MUSIAL, AN EMBLEM OF ESTEEM FROM HIS TEAMMATES. AN OUTSTANDING ARTIST IN HIS PROFESSION; THE POSSESSOR OF MANY BASEBALL REC-ORDS; A GENTLEMAN IN EVERY SENSE OF THE WORD; ADORED AND WORSHIPED BY COUNTLESS THOUSANDS; THE PERFECT ANSWER TO A MANAGER'S PRAYERS; TO THIS WE ATTEST WITH OUR SIGNATURES.

After the Kerr incident, nobody could doubt that the Cardinals were even a whisper wrong in their esti-mate of their well-loved teammate.

CHAPTER
FOUR

TWO TORRID WEEKS

It seems like a long time ago. On Wednesday, September 17, 1941, William L. Shirer's book was selling like hotcakes. But the name of it wasn't *The Rise and Fall of the Third Reich*; it was his original *Berlin Diary*. Orson Welles, then a young genius of a movie maker, was pulling them into the neighborhood theatres with his immortal *Citizen Kane*; the Nazis threatened to shoot "hostages" in Paris; and a fiery little man named Fiorello La Guardia was renominated by the Republicans for Mayor of New York City.

But some things never seem to change: the New York Yankees were 17½ games in front of the Boston Red Sox in the American League pennant race. The National League, however, was in its usual dog fight for the flag; and the St. Louis Cardinals, under the leadership of Manager Billy Southworth, were battling with the Brooklyn Dodgers led by Leo Durocher.

The day that Stan Musial, a youngster who hadn't quite yet made it to twenty-one, squirmed into a Cardinal batter's box for the first time, the Cards trailed the Dodgers by only a single game.

Stan probably would not have made it up to the parent club in 1941 if it hadn't been for the dismal luck of the Cardinals in the fading days of the pennant race. Two of their fine outfielders — Enos "Country" Slaughter and Terry Moore — had been badly shaken up in a collision in the outfield, when both of them had the same singleness of purpose in diving for a fly ball. Slaughter emerged from the accident with a broken collarbone. Although Moore escaped with a near-miss skull fracture, he was hit on the head by a pitched ball shortly after. That meant that Manager Southworth was in dire need of another outfielder.

So Stan, who had split the 1941 season with Springfield, a Class C team in the Western Association, and Rochester, a Double A team in the International League, looked like the logical candidate to help the Cards. The youth had whaled 26 homers for Manager Ollie Vanek of Springfield, while hitting .379. Then, when he moved up to Rochester, one of the minor league's fastest teams, he batted .326.

Stan's manager at Rochester, Tony Kaufmann, another ex-major league pitcher like Dickie Kerr, was convinced Stan was the goods. He hated to lose the boy so quickly to the majors, but he knew that a talented player like this was destined to be promoted rapidly.

"He was a quick learner," recalls Kaufmann. "And he had ice water in his veins."

Kaufmann taught Stan a neat trick, that to this day he hasn't forgotten. All that the trick required was the instinct and reflexes of a panther. And Stan proved equal to the task.

It was simply this: when the third baseman charged in towards the plate on a bunt situation, the batter was charged with pushing the ball over his head. If the first baseman did the same thing the batter knocked it by him, or over him.

It took Stan no time at all to become skillful at this technique.

The first time Stan did it was against a Newark third baseman, Hank Majeski. When he came back to the bench, Kaufmann was delighted with his protégé.

"It sure worked good, didn't it?" said Tony.

"Yes," said Stan, "but it really wasn't very hard to do."

Stan wasn't trying to be a braggart. He was only telling the truth. Most things that had to be done on a baseball diamond he could do with ease. And the things he found he couldn't do he picked up with alacrity.

41

This was the kind of all-around skill that had brought him to the Cards in September 1941, to provide a breathing spell for Terry Moore.

Moore, himself, one of the greatest hustling outfielders the game has ever known, remembered that Stan had once been a pitcher for a Class D team in the minors. But the first time he encountered Musial on the Card bench in 1941 he didn't recall too much more about him.

"I know that you once pitched against us in an exhibition game," said Terry, "and I thought for a pitcher you're a pretty good hitter."

"Don't you remember anything else about me?" Stan asked him, a bit puzzled.

"Can't say that I do," answered Terry.

"Well, you ought to remember more than that," said Stan, with refreshing honesty, "because you hit a homer off me that's still traveling."

In the first game of a double-header on September 17, 1941, against the Boston Braves, at Sportsman's Park in St. Louis, Manager Southworth had played Moore in center field.

Now, in the second game, Billy decided to give Terry a well-deserved rest. Southworth looked down the Cardinal bench and his eyes rested on the tanned features of the kid from Donora.

"You're going to play right field in the second one," said Southworth.

Getting such official notice from Manager South-worth was the greatest thrill of the young ballplayer's life. But years later Stan still retained his tremendous enthusiasm for the game. He never ceased to wonder about his great, good fortune at simply being in a major league uniform and having sufficient talent to play in such fast and famous company.

"Every time I step out on a field," reminisced Stan, "I try to remember who I am and where I came from and where I started. Then I have to think, 'Me, a big-leaguer?' That's the biggest charge of my life."

For his first contest in a Cardinal uniform Stan was surrounded by an auspicious group of Redbirds. Here is the lineup he joined that September day:

> Jimmy Brown, third base
> Johnny Hopp, center field
> Stan Musial, right field
> Johnny Mize, first base
> Estel Crabtree, left field
> Creepy Crespi, second base
> Marty Marion, shortstop
> Gus Mancuso, catcher
> Max Lanier, pitcher

A man named Casey Stengel was then managing the low-down Boston Braves. He was many light-years away from the high altitude he was later to gain as pilot of the New York Yankees. But it was excellent experience for his ultimate stewardship of the hapless New York Mets, whom he had under his septuagenarian wing in their inaugural season of 1962.

Casey started the knuckle-baller Jim Tobin against the Cards. Tobin pitched like an earlier version of San Francisco's Stu Miller. He had three speeds with his knuckler: slow, slower, slowest. None of the speeds did much for anyone's batting average.

In his first try against Tobin's delivery, Stan corkscrewed himself uncertainly at the left side of home plate. His stance, which was then a rather awkward version of the famous Musial crouch that was to develop through practice and use over the years, was a welcome sight for a wise old codger like Tobin.

"This kid'll be easy for a changeup," thought Tobin. So Jim let one go and Stan practically fell all over himself trying to get a piece of the ball.

Then Jim unleashed another tantalizing knuckler and Stan unwound and delivered that most fatal of blows for a hitter: a pop to the third baseman.

But history was yet to be made that day, and it wasn't long waiting in the wings. For, in the third inning Stan again faced Tobin, this time with two Cardinals on base.

Stan looked over his right shoulder menacingly at Tobin, determined to meet the knuckler solidly. When Jim aimed one at the strike zone, Stan's bat met the ball squarely — and whoosh — it headed like a bullet towards right-center field. Stan streaked for first, then moved to second, as both runners came home on the double. The double, as things have turned out, has become a Musial trademark.

It was his first hit in the big leagues — the beginning of an avalanche of base hits that would put the records of practically all other great hitters in history to shame. Some 21 years later, Stan would have a total well in excess of 3,500, a figure surpassed by only one other magician of the bat — Ty Cobb.

That the Cards won the game, 3–2, is incidental to the fact that it marked a successful debut for Musial. Only two years before, Stan was convinced that his bad left arm would mire him for life in the minors. But now he was a chirping, high-flying Redbird.

"I guess if I hadn't been dumb and fallen on that shoulder," said Stan, "I'd have been a pitcher and never got past the Three-Eye League."

In Stan's second game he made one hit in four at bats against the Braves. And it was quite apparent that aside from the fact that Manager Southworth had a need for every able-bodied man he could muster, he was impressed with Mr. Branch Rickey's young farm product.

Even the loquacious Casey Stengel sensed, as he recalls today, that a star was being born.

"That boy didn't have the same swing he's got today," begins Casey. "He was more awkward up there than he is now. All I'd heard about him before that first game with us was that he had a bum arm and that he'd been a pitcher who had been told to grab a bat. I told my pitchers to throw him slow stuff because I thought being new around these parts he wouldn't be able to hit it. But wham! He hit it right out there!"

Others who were privileged to take a look at this blossoming star can recall that from the start he looked like a menace to all pitchers.

When the New York Giants paid a late September visit to Sportsman's Park in 1941 they still had such pitching stars as Prince Hal Schumacher and the screw-balling left-hander Carl Hubbell. Hal, who has turned to the business of selling bats to sluggers like Musial since he retired from baseball, told a tale recently of how he reacted to Stan the first time he saw him in batting practice.

"I can remember this fellow Musial when he was really a kid," began Hal. "Hubbell and I were sitting on the bench in St. Louis just cutting up in a gab fest and watching the Cards take their batting practice. Then this boy steps up there and begins hitting one ball after another on a line, a dead line, to all parts of the ball park. Up against the fence, over the roof in right field, into the stands in left field. You never saw such an exhibition.

"Then I remember poor old Hub turning to me and

saying, 'Here we are just a couple of nice old guys trying to get along with people, and look what we're up against now!' "

In Stan's third game as a big-leaguer he had a perfect day, three hits in three times at bat. He batted in one run, and hit — you guessed it — a Musial double.

Jim Dawson, a sportswriter for *The New York Times,* who had scarcely heard of Musial before he went to the ball park that day, was moved to write:

"After only three games on the big-time Musial was greeted like an idol."

On Saturday of that week Manager Southworth rested his new find, presumably so he could read over his press clippings, which already were mounting. Then on Sunday Stan was back in the Card lineup for a crucial double-header with the Chicago Cubs.

What Stan did to Cub pitching that afternoon he has done on many occasions since. But he was, after all, only a neophyte, a lame-winged pitcher in on a rain check.

In the first game, while a crowd of 26,219 cheered itself hoarse rooting for the newest hero in town, Stan banged out four hits in five times at bat. He had, as usual, two doubles, worked a double-steal with Johnny Hopp, and played left field as if he had been there all of his life.

Then, in the ninth inning, and with the score knotted at 5–5, he singled, and went to second on an infield out.

47

Coaker Triplett then topped a lazy roller to the mound. The play was made on Coaker at first, and he was safe by an eyelash. But Stan never stopped running. While catcher Clyde McCullough took his eyes off the flying Musial to watch the play on Triplett at first, Stan went into high gear. He rounded third base, his legs churning, his arms pumping. In another split second he was across home plate with the winning run, beating the slightly delayed throw from first baseman Babe Dahlgren.

Few modern ballplayers will ever try to score on an infield hit from second; even fewer succeed at it. Maury Wills may do it occasionally — and Willie Mays often has the courage and agility to try it. But Stan had shown the fans his extraordinary versatility. What's more, he had gotten away with it!

As an anticlimax Stan could put together only two hits in the second game. But he was a wizard in the field, too, even though Manager Southworth switched him to right field. He picked off one Cub try for a hit at his shoestrings; turned a somersault on another play — but still came up with the ball; and then clotheslined a throw home in plenty of time to cut off a fleeing Chicagoan at home plate.

He didn't serve supper in the clubhouse after the double victory over the Cubs. But that's about all he neglected to do that afternoon.

Southworth was moved to comment that he had rarely seen such a one-man show in his life. The one-man show was actually a misnomer, for this was only a boy performing. Imagine how he'd function when he grew up and learned something about hitting and fielding!

"He was born to play this game," said Billy.

And as the season of 1941 waned, Stan, the amazing two-week rookie, strove valiantly to keep the Cards in the race with the Dodgers.

As if to prove he was more or less human Stan finally was stopped at the plate on September 23 by Pittsburgh's Ken Heintzelman. But the Cards were shut out that day, too. However, in the second game he knocked out three hits in four appearances.

On Thursday, September 25 — dark, black Thursday for the Birds — the Cards were eliminated from the pennant fight, as they lost to Pittsburgh, 3–1. But rookie Stan went two for four that day.

In a dozen ball games Musial had arrived with a bang that was heard and cheered around the baseball world. It was an introduction to the sport that few other rookies have ever equaled. Stan had come up to bat, full of vigor and a desire to help a team that had been crippled by late-season injuries, and had amassed a mark of 20 hits in 47 times at bat.

In an article for *Collier's,* written in 1947, Kyle Crichton summed up Stan's debut:

The Brooklyn Dodgers were winning their first pennant under

Leo Durocher, and the Cards were breathing on their napes at every step. Every game during those last days was a national crisis and Musial was thrown as a sacrifice into this den of tigers. In 12 spectacular games he batted .426 and almost saved the pennant for Mr. Sam Breadon, Mr. Billy Southworth and the eager St. Louis rooters . . .

CHAPTER
FIVE

ROOKIE OF THE YEAR

Stan Musial was the Rookie of the Year in 1942.
But it didn't come easy.

He had come to the Cardinals' spring training camp
in St. Petersburg, Florida, as one of the most highly
praised and ballyhooed of young players. On the heels
of his great contribution to the Cards in the fading days
of the 1941 flag fight this was only natural. But it
worked a great hardship on the youngster.

One day when Stan took a walk with a newspaperman he said wistfully, "I just hope I can stay up here a
couple of years." It was the understatement of that
spring, if not all springs.

Yet, the way life started out in 1942 for Stan it
seemed there might be reason for his self-doubt.

While the press certified him as the greatest thing

since the invention of radio and insisted he couldn't miss on a St. Louis team — that already had such stars as Country Slaughter, Terry Moore, Whitey Kurowski, the Cooper brothers (Walker and Mort), Marty Marion and Jimmy Brown — Stan reacted as any inexperienced youth might. He pressed to the limit in a desire to live up, in every way, to his press paeans.

But the more he tried and the more he pressed, the less certain he became in the field and at bat.

For one thing his bad left shoulder, the one that had almost reduced him to a Class D ballplayer in perpetuity, started to act up on him again. The word got around the spring training camps that Stan Musial couldn't throw very much. So when the Cards pulled into town for an exhibition game the runners tried him out and he didn't do particularly well.

That was the least of the young man's troubles, however. For the .426 hitter of 1941's final two weeks had turned into a soft touch at the plate. Most of the pitchers, good, bad and indifferent, were getting him out easily. He popped up, struck out, topped manageable grounders to the infield.

Manager Southworth, keenly aware of the pressure Stan was under, now refused to knuckle under to the demands of the fickle fans and writers.

"This kid is only a morning glory," the scoffers began to say. And Billy Southworth had been around long enough to know that baseball invariably produced its roster of "paper stars." They came to prominence over-night, received wild acclaim from the press, then disappeared as quickly as they had risen. Could Stan be one of those unfortunate cases?

The more Billy watched the weak arm, the lunges at the plate, the all-around futility, the more he could be justified in feeling that perhaps the boy just didn't have it, that 1941 had been one of those horrible mistakes.

"I just couldn't see the ball in those weeks back in 1942 at spring training," Stan has said. "If I hadn't had that great start in 1941 I'm sure the team never would have taken me North with them. They would have been justified in forgetting about me. But they had seen that I could hit a little when I first came up."

It is to Southworth's credit that he never really gave up on Stan. Yes, he was astounded at the change in the boy. But he understood the forces that were acting against the youngster's best interests.

"He's trying to bang a homer every time he gets a bat in his hands," mused Billy. "When he stops doing that he'll be fine. He has too much baseball instinct to fail."

Finally the manager made one concession to the detractors: he benched Stan for a few days. Then he brought the boy back against right-handed pitchers, bowing for a moment to baseball's percentage law. The strategy seemed to pay off. The southpaw-swinging Musial started to knock right-handers all over the place.

Then, graduating against righties, Stan was allowed to appear in the lineup again against all kinds of pitchers.

Slowly but surely, under the relaxed and restrained vigilance of his wise manager, Stan came around. Now the only question that remained was whether or not Stan would be in the starting lineup at the opening of the season. And if he was, just where would he play?

Southworth didn't make anyone wait long for his answer. He announced that Stan was going to be his left fielder.

There was some impolite talk about this maneuver in the more orthodox baseball circles, for it was traditional for a right-handed thrower to patrol left field. The reasoning, which may have some validity, is that a right-handed outfielder wears his glove on his left hand, which thus protects the field, rather than the foul line. Have you ever stopped to think how many southpaws you have seen playing left field in the majors?

However, Billy refused to be stampeded by such reasoning. "He can make the plays upside down out there," Southworth insisted.

Supported by his manager's unflinching confidence in him, Stan made up his mind not to fail.

As the regular season progressed Stan was making the plays, just as his manager had predicted he would. He was more than satisfactory in the field, as he tumbled and scrambled for line drives. And when runners tested that "weak" arm, relying on the persistent reports that it wasn't strong enough to throw out fleet base runners like themselves, they were surprised to wind up in a cloud of dust with an umpire flashing the "out" sign.

True, the one impediment in Musial's armor has turned out to be the arm. But it was good enough in 1942 to make the runners respect him. They simply stopped taking liberties, which is all Southworth could have hoped for.

"If there's any single regret I've ever had about my baseball career," Stan said a few years ago, "it's that I had to play without my good arm. Through the years I always had that weakness. Of course, as long as I was hitting well, I never did worry about my arm too much, and early in my career I had a little more speed and a little more zip. I could charge the ball quicker. Then my weakness through the arm injury wasn't too noticeable. But I always wished I could have thrown a bit better."

At bat Stan, although not quite as sensational as he had been in 1941, began to hit with increasing consistency. By the season's end he had a neat .315 average, including 32 doubles, ten home runs, and 72 runs batted in.

As the pennant race developed into another Donnybrook with the Dodgers, Stan more and more became the key figure in the Card lineup. He out-hit Terry Moore by some 27 points and Country Slaughter only had a three-point edge on him when the schedule was concluded. But, more important, he delivered base hits when they were needed.

If anyone had ever had doubts about his ability and his courage — as they had for those few frustrating months during the spring — they could dispel them now, for Stan had shown that he was for real.

In August and September, as the Cards battled the Dodgers tooth and nail, Musial led the way. The Birds had been 10 games behind the Brooklyn team as late as August 6. But Southworth refused to give up, and so did his hustling, aggressive ball club, which was, in so many ways, a fit successor to the hilarious Gashouse Gang of the thirties.

By winning 43 of its final 52 games, the Cards eked out their comeback pennant over Brooklyn.

The Cards won 106 games and the Dodgers 104. That gave them a two-game edge. It also put Stan Musial, who had contributed so much, into the first of the four World Series — 1942, 1943, 1944, 1946 —that he would play in a St. Louis uniform.

CHAPTER SIX

THE RECORD BREAKER

In many respects Stan Musial is the most remarkable batter ever to have played in a National League uniform. You won't get into an argument with too many baseball fans if you make the flat assertion that nobody — including Rogers Hornsby, Mel Ott or Honus Wagner — was any better. If you include such American League greats as Ty Cobb, Babe Ruth, Ted Williams or Joe DiMaggio, you might find yourself in the middle of a verbal tussle. But even there you will find that your debating opponent harbors a soft spot in his heart for the quiet slugger from St. Louis.

Warren Giles, who is by no means without a professional bias in Stan's favor, since he is paid to be president of the National League, insists that Musial is the "greatest all-around ballplayer ever to wear a uniform." That statement takes in a large chunk of territory. Yet for those who have been privileged to watch this splendid and versatile competitor, there is a strong tendency to agree with Mr. Giles.

Records, which are to the average baseball fan the true lifeline of the game, provide solid support for Giles and those others who find Stan Musial unequaled in his profession. Perhaps it is true that the steady listing of records that Stan has broken over the years may have dulled somewhat an appreciation of his skills, simply through excessive repetition of the obvious. However, it is always worth reviewing some of the man's major accomplishments.

He has led his league in batting seven times. He has been the Most Valuable Player in his league three times. He has made over 200 hits six times. He has batted over .300, the mark that is generally accepted as the dividing line between hitters and non-hitters, 18 times, including a remarkable average of .330, in the 1962 season, his 21st year in baseball. He has batted in over 100 runs 10 times. His lifetime average is well above .330.

We will skip the multitude of other records that he holds, has broken and did break practically every time he rolled up his socks during the 1962 season. We will not go into the complicated mathematical formulae that were used by one admirer of Stan's to fix the number of miles — 132 plus — that Musial has hit baseballs to reach his plateau of over 3,500 hits.

These statistics only help to tell the story. They help to affirm the fact that any way you look at Stan he is a baseball genius, a true once-in-a-lifetime player.

Strangely, a half-ironic, half-serious remark that was dropped by a Houston pitcher in 1962, comes as close as anything ever said or written about Stan to place him in the proper perspective.

After facing Musial one night, Dick Farrell, a big, fast-balling right-hander, conceded that he had thrown a spitball in Stan's direction. Or, as he later corrected it, a sweatball.

"But he lined it for a single, anyway," moaned Farrell. "You can't even get that fellow out on an illegal pitch."

For years — 21 to be exact — the National League's pitchers have been faced with the same inflexible problem: How to get The Man out.

He has, almost from the day he faced pitcher Jim Tobin in his freshman year, meandered into combat, unhurried, poised, determined. Then he has proceeded to square off on the left-hander's side of the plate, bat held high above his head and left shoulder, hips and shoulders wiggling and waggling as if he invented the

Twist himself, knees bent in a relaxed crouch, in what is undoubtedly one of the most unorthodox stances ever used by any hitter in history.

Of course there have been other hitters, some of them successful, who have employed odd and peculiar stances. For years, over in the American League, Al Simmons lashed out viciously at all pitchers with his left foot planted plunk in the bucket, in defiance of all sound baseball theory. There were players like Heinie Groh and Wally Moses who practically faced the pitcher when they batted. Others like Frankie Frisch have hit cross-handed while Master Melvin Ott hit, as one observer has suggested, like a penguin, off one leg, while his right foot was high in the air. Then Pete Gray, a man with only one arm, hit, of course, with one arm.

But compared to all of these stances or approaches, Musial's still has to be the most eye-catching and certainly the most confounding.

In Stan's first season, when some usually sharp-eyed observers had a chance to see his unorthodox technique for the first time, they shook their heads sadly.

"The boy can't hit up here with that stance," they clucked, "he'll have to change it."

"He doesn't look like a hitter, except when he is hitting," once cracked the late Bill Corum, the columnist from Missouri, who always acknowledged he was a Cardinal fan.

Stan, a man who has always listened eagerly to his

peers, and certainly to anyone for whom he has respect, simply ignored such comments. The stance, which to some might have seemed ludicrous, crude and uncomfortable, served his purposes to the nth degree. It enabled him to feel a maximum of ease and comfort when hitting; and if it did cause some to doubt its value at the start, within a decade it was easily the most feared and familiar posture in baseball.

No pitcher has ever quite come up with a solution to curb its success, although some of the smartest of them have tried. When he was still pitching for the Brooklyn Dodgers, "Preacher" Roe prescribed one particular formula, which was the highest kind of tribute to Stan.

"The best way to handle this fellow," suggested Preacher, who was an Arkansas philosopher from head to toe, "is to throw him four quick wide ones. Then you've got a fighting chance to pick him off first base."

There have been many quips made about Stan's hula wiggle stance at home plate. Some have compared it to a dancer pirouetting in a ballet. Others have said it reminded them of a cobra coiling to strike or a bow string drawn to a maximum of tautness. One that I particularly like suggests that Musial hunches there at the plate, with big number 6 on his back, somewhat like a relaxed and retiring question mark.

Perhaps the most widely quoted description of Stan's stance is the one attributed to Ted Lyons, who pitched for many years for the Chicago White Sox.

"He looks," said Lyons, "like a kid peeking around the corner to see if the cops are coming."

Musial has performed enough mayhem on National League pitching to warrant calling out the cops. But that's what he has been paid to do (up to $100,000 per year, as a matter of fact) and nobody has suggested, since 1941, that he trade in his cock-eyed approach to moundsmen for a new model.

Somewhat drolly, the great southpaw Warren Spahn said, while watching Stan tee off in batting practice prior to the 1961 All-Star Game at San Francisco, "You should change that dang style of yours. It'll never do you any good, son."

Stan, who has a good-natured grin that splits his face like a watermelon slice, laughed out loud at Spahn's remark.

"I'm afraid it's too late to change," replied Stan. "You can't teach an old dog new tricks."

CHAPTER SEVEN

SECRETS OF HITTING

A few years ago, as a night train sped from St. Louis to another baseball destination, Stan Musial was talking about his favorite subject — batting — to Roger Kahn, a perceptive sports reporter and magazine writer. Nobody in baseball in recent years, with the possible exception of Ted Williams, who could safely be awakened in the middle of the night to talk shop about hitting, has put in as much time and attention on the subject as Stan.

Kahn was trying to account for Stan's ability, even at an advanced baseball age, to hit all kinds of pitching with more than reasonable success.

"I never guess at what the pitch is going to be,"

Musial said, without a trace of braggadocio. "I just know what the pitch is going to be."

"You really know?" said Kahn, surprised.

"Yes, I think so," said Stan.

"At what point do you know?"

"When the pitch gets about halfway to home plate," answered Stan.

"How do you tell, by the way the ball is rotating?" asked Kahn.

"No," said Musial, weighing his words carefully, for now he was revealing one of the true secrets of his two decades of greatness as a hitter. "Every pitcher has his set of speeds. The curve, for instance, comes in at one speed, the slider comes in at another, the knuckler at another. Well, you see, if I concentrate real hard I can pick up the speed of the ball about the first 30 feet it travels. I know the pitcher and I know his speeds. So when I really concentrate halfway in I usually know what the pitch is going to do, how the ball is going to move, when it gets up to the plate."

"Are you always in a concentrating mood?" asked Kahn, realizing he had truly discovered a significant thread to Stan's skill as a batter.

"Well, I always try to concentrate," replied Stan, "but sometimes I don't do it as well as other times. When I'm tired physically I become mentally tired, too. That's only natural, isn't it? I think when I was really in my prime I could concentrate on practically every pitch.

But in recent years my ability to concentrate has decreased some."

Stan then went on to point out that his occasional lapses in concentration had undoubtedly cost him plenty of points on his batting averages.

"When I think of the times I didn't concentrate," said Musial, "it gets me sore. I know that when a ballplayer has been playing an awful lot, he has to have a letdown. But you can't afford to swing at balls just to be swinging. You've got to know what you're doing and why you're doing it if you expect to have any kind of a batting average and win ball games with your hits."

Few players, of course, have been able to concentrate as completely and devotedly as Stan. But the point he makes, as simple as it sounds, is the key to a transcendent performance in almost any sport you can name — golf, tennis, football, even water skiing.

In Stan's case utter and total concentration on hitting a baseball — "you've got to center your bat on the ball every time you swing" — has produced remarkable dividends, in the form of large salaries, national acclaim and the satisfaction of knowing within himself that he is an acknowledged expert at his craft.

But if you examine his theory, his hitting operation even more closely — and you have to believe what he says, for he is no charlatan — he emerges as one of the few true wizards ever to challenge a pitcher's right to blaze a ball past his ever-threatening bat.

Spring training always includes calisthenics to limber up muscles gone flabby over the winter. Stan is laughing, not grimacing.

In effect, Stan, after deciding exactly what the pitch is going to be, adjusts his swing to hit it about three-tenths of a second before it reaches the hands of the catcher.

Since there are always some 90 pitchers operating in the National League (with the 10-team loop setup the figure would have to be closer to 100 pitchers), and each pitcher presumably functions with a repertoire of three to five different deliveries, that means that Musial reduces to memory anywhere from 300 to 500 pitches. This is an achievement that would even challenge the prodigious memory of an expert mathematician, as well as a modern T-quarterback in professional football.

It is quite obvious that over the years nobody has really ever learned how to pitch to Stan. When Casey Stengel managed the Boston Braves in the early years of Musial's career, he named pitcher Red Barrett one afternoon to face the Cards.

When Stan's turn came to face Barrett, Casey hopped out of the dugout to suggest that a tantalizing slow pitch might be just what the doctor ordered for the young upstart.

"He'll pop it up," said Casey reassuringly, as he returned to his bench position.

But even before Stengel had a chance to settle himself in the dugout, Musial pounced on Barrett's first pitch — a slow one, of course — and practically buried it in the next county.

Barrett was disenchanted, to say the least.

"You don't know anything about pitching to this guy," snapped the hurler, after the inning was over.

When a reporter refreshed Stengel's memory about the incident last year, his rubbery face broke into a thousand creases.

"You know something," he mused. "Barrett was right — and nobody knows how to pitch to him now, either."

The fear that Musial has engendered around the league among the pitching fraternity has always been a genuine thing. No baseball press agent has had to talk it up to sell tickets. The simple truth is that as one of the true students of hitting in baseball's long history, Stan has become one of the sharpest analysts of pitching technique and ball park architecture within the memory of any observer.

"I don't like to do anything I can't do well," Stan has said. "I guess you'd call me a perfectionist. I'm a ballplayer. I hit the ball well. That's what I like to do."

Not only is Stan a self-styled perfectionist, but he is also a reasonable man, who has used a calm, easy-going disposition to full advantage in his profession.

There have been other perfectionists in the game, too. But they have not fared as well as Stan, simply because they would, on occasion, become inflexible in their attitude.

A notable example, of course, is Ted Williams. Ted was a keen student of everything that had to do with connecting with a baseball, and he is a sure-fire Hall of Famer, as is Stan. But there is no telling how much greater he might have been had he not directly challenged a system — the "Williams shift" — that was deliberately set up to thwart his hitting efforts.

The Williams shift could only flourish because Ted was stubborn enough to ram his head against it. Manager Lou Boudreau of the Cleveland Indians, who devised the stratagem to haze and hinder Ted, knew enough about Ted's personality to anticipate that the great hitter would not try to hit to left field, if Lou's fielders were all deployed on the right side of the diamond. That's the kind of man Ted was.

But Stan Musial is *not* that kind of a man.

If a "Musial shift" had ever been put into play against his southpaw stance, he would simply have hit to left and center fields. As it is, he has always been known in the trade as a "spray hitter," which means he is thoroughly capable of confounding any defense that is contrived to stop him.

If a good hitter must learn, insists Stan, to hit to all fields, he must also learn to hit in all parks.

"The good batter," he once told sportswriter Red Smith, "tries to adjust himself to the park he's playing in. These kids who just stand up there and swing, they're hitting the pitch that the pitcher wants 'em to hit. They knock it a mile to left or to right center and it winds up as nothing but a big out. A good hitter tries to measure the park he's in."

This is accomplished, says Stan, by the way the batter swings.

"If the pitch is inside and fast, you try to hit it out in front of the plate and pull to right. If it's outside, you swing late and try to slice it to left field."

Giving a specific example, Stan cited the Polo Grounds, which was used last year for the last time in its ancient history by the forlorn New York Mets.

"I tried to pull everything to right field there," said Stan. "I'd usually lay off outside pitches. Or even if it was outside I'd whip my wrists through and try to pull it."

The Polo Grounds, of course, has always, along with Brooklyn's Ebbets Field, been Musial's favorite hitting stadium. He truthfully mourned the passing of both from the National League scene.

Youngsters eager to learn the finer points of hitting could do well to take a course under Stan. For not only has he applied his own findings and research to practical use — seven National League batting titles, for example — but he is extremely articulate in discussing the subject. But with it all there is a clarity and simplicity about his dissection of the batting art that has probably never had a peer among the game's great batters.

"The main thing when you bat," says Stan, "is to hold that bat back, always ready. You never commit yourself — or your bat. By that I mean you should never let your bat go out until you know whether it's a fast ball or a curve or a changeup. Your bat should be back, so that whatever kind of pitch it turns out to be, you still can hit that ball with power. A lot of batters commit themselves entirely too soon. They commit their arms and their bodies. They commit their swings. If it doesn't turn out to be the pitch they're looking for, they just don't have any power left."

Surprisingly, perhaps, Stan maintains that a good fast ball is still the toughest pitch for a batter to hit.

"It's hard to center on a good fast one," he says, "because some pitchers have a fast ball that rises, or moves around a lot."

As a performer who owns a lifetime batting average, over 21 seasons, in excess of .330, Musial is often asked to philosophize about the so-called "declining art" of hitting. What he has said makes a good deal of common sense and is worth repeating, especially his theories about night baseball and the equipment used by the moderns.

"I really think the night game has cut a lot of points off batting averages," Stan says, "because they can't do anything about lighting up the background for the ball park. The skies, the outside buildings, the trees. They're all in blackness. So a batter loses his sense of depth perception.

"The gloves, too, work against the hitter today. They're all bigger and better made. Some of the plays these fielders make today with these gloves you wouldn't see once in a season when I was a rookie in this game."

But Stan Musial refuses to go along with the well-worn theory that the old days were better. He doesn't have that traditional nostalgia for the past that is so commonplace among so many of baseball's irascible greats, like the Hornsbys, the Cobbs and the Frankie Frischs.

"The players," says Stan, with a ring of sincerity, "are just as good now as they were then. The only difference is in the game. There will always be super-stars to replace the super-stars of yesterday."

What Stan The Man neglected to add is that there will never be any such individual to replace himself.

CHAPTER EIGHT

THEY CALL HIM "THE MAN"

Before the real estate operators of Brooklyn made up their minds to hack down the revered portals of Ebbets Field, they should have earnestly consulted Stan Musial.

For it was here, in this cozy crazyhouse of a baseball arena, that Musial, a man who had countless great days at the plate, registered some of his finest artistic successes. There were many seasons when Stan would come away from playing his 11 games at old Ebbets with a batting average of over .500.

One day, in the years before Mr. Walter O'Malley pulled his Dodgers out of Ebbets Field and planted them in the backyard of the film colony, several cele-

Spry at 36, Stan lopes playfully in the outfield during spring training in St. Petersburg, Florida, before the 1957 season.

brated baseball figures were discussing with Stan his incredible play in Brooklyn's ball orchard.

"Have you hit any balls against that right-field screen this year?" asked Leo Durocher, who was then still engaged as the manager of the New York Giants.

Someone took it upon himself to answer for Stan. "He only hits them *over* the screen," was the comment.

"You're not kidding," roared Durocher. "If Stan played in Brooklyn all the time he'd hit close to 1.000!"

"What's the secret, Stan?" one of the group asked. "How do you do it?"

"It's a small park, I guess," was Stan's humble reply.

"But you get plenty of hits that don't go outside the park or rattle the fences," insisted the questioner. "Lots of your hits are inside the park."

Stan could answer only with a shrug and a smile. Even if he knew the answer he wasn't about to give out any more trade secrets.

But when the subject was brought up, he couldn't help but remember vividly an awesome demonstration of skill and power that he had staged in May 1948 at Ebbets Field.

In that three-game series with the Dodgers Stan hung up the blistering total of 11 base hits in 15 times at bat, for a .733 pace. He smashed five doubles, one triple and one home run, as well as four singles.

In the first game of the set Stan went two for four, thus warming up slowly to his task. The next night,

Wednesday, before some 32,000 bug-eyed Brooklyn fans, Stan delivered five hits in five appearances and scored five times. The Cards managed to win, 14–7. Then the next day, just to add icing to the cake, Stan swished out four more hits in six times up, to become a legend in the borough of Brooklyn.

"Even Musial admits he's not that good," wrote Dick Young of the New York *Daily News,* after Musial had finished with his one-man carnage.

Leo Durocher, as the manager of the Dodgers, was the victim of Musial's attack. But he couldn't contain his praise of the player who had drubbed his pitchers silly.

"I've seen some great hitters in my time," said the lippy Dodger pilot, "but I've never seen a hotter hitter over a three-day period than Musial was in this series. Time and again our pitchers would get ahead of him. They'd get two strikes on him. Then the agony would start. He'd foul off three or four good pitches. Then our fellow would make a mistake — and away it went!

"Why, that man made the fences of this park look as close as the walls of this office!"

It was at Ebbets Field, too, that Stan's simple, but respectful nickname of "The Man" was first used, almost out of wonderment and fear.

"Here comes The Man again," one of the Flatbush faithful mumbled one day, as the player proudly bear-

76

ing the big number six on his back carved out his position in the batter's box.

And the nickname has stuck, with the certainty of glue.

If The Man has experienced some of his most unforgettable batting days at Ebbets Field, he has certainly never confined his brilliance to that field. That is one of the things that has made Stan so truly great.

Some years ago, when Joe Reichler, a baseball reporter, was putting together a book devoted to the outstanding individual accomplishments of famous players, Stan was asked what he thought his greatest day had been. The event he chose — and this was before Stan knocked out his 3,000th base hit — was the day, in September 1948, when he smashed out five hits in five times at bat, to mark the fourth time that year he had performed the feat. By doing so he tied Ty Cobb's all-time mark of four five-hit games.

However, what made Stan's performance that afternoon at Braves Field against the Boston Braves so matchless, was that he was not operating at anything approaching his peak efficiency. In addition, he was batting against the talented southpaw Warren Spahn, who was seeking to give his team the one victory it needed to sew up a pennant.

Only a few days before, while playing in Ebbets Field, Stan had jammed his left wrist in the process of making a couple of circus catches against the Dodgers. As if that wasn't enough his right wrist was nicked by one of Carl Erskine's pitches in the same series. So, going into the game on September 22, with the Braves, Stan was hurting badly. He refused, however, to permit Doc Weaver to bandage his wrists. Instead, he insisted that he play, as usual, as the Braves sought to wrap up the flag.

As the game got under way Stan fully realized that his wrists presented a distinct handicap at the plate. He couldn't snap them in order to pull the ball to right field, and he was having a good deal of trouble taking a firm grip on his bat.

The first time he faced Spahn, before 11,000 people on this typical fall day, he nudged a single into left field. He didn't really have to snap his wrists to hit in that direction and he thought he would try the same thing the next time up, too.

In the third inning, with Spahn still in the game, Stan popped one over the left fielder's head for a two-bagger.

In the fourth inning, Red Barrett, a right-hander, had come on to relieve Spahn. It was now, for the first time that afternoon, that Stan decided, despite the pain, to swing hard. He did, and the ball went rocketing into the stands for a home run.

With three hits in three times up under his belt, Stan faced another Braves relief man, Clyde Shoun, in the sixth inning. Shoun obliged Stan by throwing him a soft, outside pitch which he carefully pushed into left field, just out of the reach of the Boston shortstop, who happened to be Al Dark that day.

Players are not always thoroughly conversant with the record books. That chore is left to the TV announcers and the press box computers, who sometimes may be safely accused of turning baseball into a dreary numbers game — which it most certainly is not. But Stan was aware of the Ty Cobb record of getting five hits in four games in a single season. And he was now quite eager to carry on his assault, however painful it might be to him, against the fifth Boston pitcher, righthander Al Lyons.

His chance came soon enough, for the Cards had their batting clothes on and players kept parading to the plate.

When Stan connected against Lyons, it was not a screeching liner or a towering homer, but a routine ground ball toward right field. But it went through safely for a hit — and that made five for the day.

The most amazing element about the day, however, was not that he managed to share a record with Cobb that had stood for 26 years. It was, as Joe Reichler and Ben Olan point out in their book *Baseball's Unforgettable Games,* that Musial had decided that since the pain was so intense he couldn't afford to waste any swings. So what did he do? He made five hits on just five swings of his bat!

There were no fouls, no missed strikes.

That day Stan Musial could not squander the strength that he had left in his wrists.

Although Musial and many other ballplayers continue to regard the annual All-Star Game as a simple exhibition game, the true competitors still give it the old college try. And Stan is no exception. He goes all out whenever he is on a ball field.

In 1955, a year that did not turn out to be one of Stan's best, by a long shot, he broke up the All-Star contest, played in Milwaukee, with a 12th inning home run off Frank Sullivan's first pitch.

It was a particularly gratifying turn of events for Stan, because that year he wasn't even voted as a starting member of the National League team.

Strangely, it was also Stan's first homer of the year in the Milwaukee ball park. But even more important was the fact that the game-winning blast inaugurated something of a legend.

The legend — similar to the one about Babe Ruth pointing to the center-field bleachers in Chicago in the 1932 World Series and then hitting the ball there — says that Stan also made an advance prediction that he was going to hit his homer. Stan himself had denied that he did any such thing. He is the kind of man who is instantly willing to set the record straight, especially when it is in need of straightening.

In this instance, Stan has insisted, he merely went up

to the plate "with the idea of meeting one of Sullivan's fast balls and getting on base."

The legend, however, did spring from a chat that actually took place as Stan took his position at the plate at the start of the inning.

Yogi Berra of the Yankees was behind the bat at the time and he rarely misses an opportunity to engage in sparkling conversation with the opposition.

"Boy, am I bushed," said Yogi, as Stan stepped in.

"I'm getting pretty tired, too," said Stan.

"My feet are killing me," Yogi grumbled.

Stan, always accommodating, then said, "Maybe I can put you out of your misery."

When the remark was later relayed to the press it was immediately hailed as a Stan Musial prediction of a homer. Thus, the legend has grown, without much debunking, out of that informal exchange of remarks.

Rarely, perhaps, has there been an All-Star home run greeted with as much unmitigated joy as this one that Stan delivered.

"I crossed my fingers for Stan when he came to bat in the twelfth," said Mrs. Musial, who was at the game, "and it sure helped, didn't it?"

Warren Giles, the National League president, couldn't help but recall that the last extra-inning game of the All-Star series, a 14-inning affair in 1950, was won by Red Schoendienst's home run. Red, of course, had been Stan's roommate for years.

Giles was all smiles when he shook hands with Stan in the National League dressing room.

"If it's not one Cardinal it's another," he said. "Congratulations."

"Thank you, sir," said Stan.

Later, in writing his impressions of the homer, Jimmy Cannon, the New York columnist, said:

He is a quiet man who doesn't milk applause with vaudeville flamboyance. He always appears to be embarrassed by adulation. He never showboats. He isn't an umpire-baiter or a big mouth guy who talks down the other teams. He does it all with his big bat and his glove. . . . He isn't as fast as he used to be. But I'll take him in a crisis. I don't care who is pitching, either. Neither does Musial.

The final tribute came from Leo Durocher, who managed the National League All-Stars that year.

While players were celebrating Musial's blast in no uncertain terms and the noise even tended to drown out his own strident voice, Durocher hoarsely shouted:

"The guy owed me that one. He's killed me a hundred different times. He killed me five times in one day last year — that one he owed me."

Durocher was referring, of course, to another monumental hitting day in Stan's career. The Giants, who were to go on to win the pennant in 1954, were in St. Louis on Sunday, May 2, that year. It was a pleasant spring day and 27,000 fans journeyed to Busch Stadium for what they hoped would be two victories for the home club.

They had to settle, instead, for a single win, for the Cards lost the second game. But they were presented with the added bonus of Stan Musial at his absolute hitting peak. For, during the afternoon, Musial hit five home runs, thus etching his name in the record books as the first man in history to accomplish this feat of long-distance clouting.

The irony of this Musial record is that he has never truthfully considered himself a home run hitter in the tradition of the Babe Ruths or Lou Gehrigs or Mel Otts or Mickey Mantles or Ralph Kiners or Willie Mayses. There is no denying that Stan has hit 463 homers in his career and that he has hit as many as 39 homers in a single season (1948). But in his own mind Stan is a line-drive hitter, a "singles guy," who doesn't really try for all the marbles when he faces a pitcher.

But, against an array of Giant pitchers that May day, he was a demon. Those weren't refugees from the Little League that Stan faced that day, either. For he hit two home runs off Johnny Antonelli, who was an outstanding 20-game southpaw for the Giants that year, as well as a star in the World Series sweep over the Cleveland Indians.

He hit two also against the puzzling knuckle-ball delivery of Hoyt Wilhelm, who was an indispensable bull pen operative for the New Yorkers in those years, before he moved on to other ports and other successes. The other homer was rifled off Jim Hearn, the big right-hander who had helped the Giants so considerably in the famous 1951 flag drive against the Brooklyn Dodgers.

All in all, it was a show to remember.

After Stan had succeeded in hitting his fourth homer (he also had one single and two walks for the day, as well as nine runs batted in), he was informed, less than casually by the St. Louis press and several of his teammates, that if he hit one more home run for the day he would have himself a record.

"When I heard that I decided to go for another homer," recalls Stan. "Usually I don't go for homers, but this was a spot I thought I would try for it."

So it was in the seventh inning of the second game that Stan got his big chance and made good on it. Wilhelm was pitching at the time. The meaty Giant relief pitcher, who had been pasted for a homer by Stan in the fifth inning, scarcely was in a mood to help Musial with his record.

Hoyt threw two knucklers to Stan. The first one came twirling and dancing to the plate and Stan didn't offer at it. The second fell victim to the artful swishing swing of the Cardinals' star.

"It was a good one," says Stan. "It went way over the right-field pavilion."

With five home runs already in his trunk, Musial

received one final opportunity, in the ninth inning, to better his own mark. Facing another able Giant right-hander, Larry Jansen (who is now a pitching coach for the San Francisco Giants), Stan definitely decided to go for the home run again. It is well to keep in mind the fact that Musial has only on a few, rare occasions attempted to hit a ball out of a park.

"I just don't swing for the fence," says Stan. "I've done it only four or five times that I can remember, and that last time up against the Giants was one time I was really up there with that in mind."

The best Stan could do in this case was raise a pop-up to first baseman Whitey Lockman. But it was a pop-up that drew a grin from Stan — and from most of the fans who cheered his every effort that afternoon.

Unfortunately for Stan, his wife Lil, who tries to make every home game that Stan plays in, was not on hand to see him on his "great day." And neither was Dick, his son, who also appears in the St. Louis park to see his Dad whenever he can.

But only a few seconds after the day's work was done Lil was on the phone to congratulate her husband. Mrs. Musial keeps close tabs on the Cardinals, and especially on her husband's daily performance, and she is a wonderful, knowledgeable rooting section all by herself.

When Stan arrived home, Dick pretended he hadn't heard about the events of the day. Then, when he was

85

forced to acknowledge his father's Herculean batting chore, Dick, with the same kind of teasing good nature that is so typical of his famous dad, pooh-poohed the bag of five homers.

"Heck, Dad," said young Dick, who has since graduated from Notre Dame, "what kind of pitchers could Mr. Durocher have been using today? Can you even remember their names?"

"Well," said Stan, "you should have been there to see it. It was great fun."

"I'd like to see you do it again tomorrow," said Dick. "Then I'll believe it's for real."

"All I can do is try," said Stan, laughing and throwing his arm around his son.

Stan did try the next day, too. But the Giant pitchers were hardly as cooperative as they'd been on gloomy Sunday. They devised a simple formula for checking Stan's ambitions: they walked him four times. The only time he hit the ball was in the second inning, when he was permitted to foul out.

It is interesting, as well as remarkable, that eight years after Stan threw the Giant pitching staff into fits with his five-homer exhibition, he set to work on another menagerie of pitchers who also happen to be tenants at the Polo Grounds. This time, of course, Stan picked on the hurlers of the New York Mets. And this time Stan was a mere stripling of forty-one years of age, a total of years that is generally associated in baseball with pension plans and dreams of retirement.

On July 7, 1962, Stan defeated the Mets by hitting a home run off Craig Anderson. Then the next day, a Sunday (Stan has earned a reputation for being an excellent Sunday hitter, but he hits so well at all times it is difficult to stamp him as a hitter who hits better on certain days of the week), The Man really unloaded. He hit three straight home runs, two off right-hander Jay Hook and one off left-hander Willard Hunter. Counting the homer the previous day, that made four straight homers for the old fellow.

Once again this was one of those situations where the facts became compelling for The Man. Confronted by the record-breaking possibilities, as he came to bat in the eighth inning, with the Cards protecting a long lead, Stan elected to try for a fifth consecutive homer. The crowd applauded him vigorously as he assumed his ineffable stance at the plate. Spitefully they rooted against their own boy, Bob Miller. Then the shouts and cheers evaporated into a hush, as the veteran peered into Miller's eyes.

When the first two pitches by Miller were high, wide and balls, the crowd let the Met pitcher know in no uncertain terms that they wanted Stan to have a chance to hit. So Miller obliged. He threw the next one right down the middle and Stan just looked at it, balefully.

Then Stan swung at a low-breaking pitch for strike two. With the count at two and two, Stan took a hitch at his belt, then stepped back into the batter's box. Miller's next pitch was a curve, low and into the dirt. But Stan was eager and went for it, for the third strike. If there was a comical aspect to the situation it was that Stan wound up on first when the errant pitch got past the Mets' catcher, Chris Cannizzaro.

"I guess I was a little too anxious," Stan said later in the dressing room, as the sportswriters gathered around him, seeking angles and new things to say about a man of whom they had said practically everything there is to say.

One writer, Howard Tuckner of *The New York Times,* did succeed admirably in typing out a novel approach to the problem.

He wrote: "There's no doubt about it, and it's a great pity. At the age of forty-one, Stan Musial is all washed up. He struck out on a wild pitch in the eighth inning yesterday."

And Stan, in his own mild, modest way, tried to agree with Tuckner. "Yes," he nodded, "I looked terrible on that one. It was the only time I tried for a homer today, too."

Unlike the time in 1954 when he had hit his last three homers in one game, Stan had his favorite rooter in the park for this prime event. Lil had come to New

York primarily to show twelve-year-old Janet, her daughter, some of the more interesting New York sights.

But to the Musials the most interesting sight still happens to be Stan Musial waving his magic wand of a bat. So Lil and Janet were in the Polo Grounds to thrill to their favorite ballplayer's demonstration of batting prowess.

"I'm glad Janet and I decided to come to the ball game," said Lil.

All of these big batting days have provided Stan Musial with thrills. But he has had so many productive games, so many astoundingly good afternoons and nights since 1941, that it would be unfair to tax him to pin it down to the single game that he remembers most fondly.

It is typical of Stan's attitude towards baseball, an attitude shared so understandingly by his mother, that when she was once rushed to the hospital straight from the Pittsburgh ball park, she insisted that her son not be told until after the game.

"If they told him about me," said Stan's mother, "he would have come right to the hospital. But I just couldn't do that to him — he was having such a good day at bat. He had two hits when I was suddenly taken ill."

Today, or any day that you approach Stan Musial and ask him what his biggest thrill has been, to date, in baseball, you will get the same answer. It is a standard, pat reply. But nobody has ever doubted its sincerity, or honesty.

"My biggest thrill," maintains Stan, "is just putting on that Cardinal uniform day after day, and feeling, in my heart, how lucky I am to play the game. I will always consider it a privilege to be in baseball."

CHAPTER NINE

THE 3,000th HIT

Some pitchers, who might ordinarily remain well-forgotten, have achieved a measure of immortality by doing the wrong thing, at the right time. Tom Zachary, a lanky farmer from North Carolina, threw up Babe Ruth's 60th home run ball in September 1927. Ralph Branca, a good-looking ex-college basketball player, unleashed *that* pitch to Bobby Thomson in the last game of the 1951 National League pennant playoff between the New York Giants and the Brooklyn Dodgers. Tracy Stallard, a 6'5" rookie right-hander for the Boston Red Sox, was on the throwing end of Roger Maris' 61st home run of the 1961 season.

The day that Stan Musial whacked out his 3,000th

hit — it was on Tuesday, May 13, 1958 — a pitcher named Moe Drabowsky became the unwilling "hero" of the moment. Moe is more apt to be remembered because he tossed up the ball that Stan turned into his 3,000th hit, than for the fact that he was once, ever so briefly, a promising pitcher for the Chicago Cubs.

Of all of Stan's multifarious records and achievements in baseball it is probably fair and truthful to say that he cherishes the record of having made his 3,000 hits more than any other.

"I want that 3,000th hit more than anything else in my life," Stan said, as he started the 1958 season, with only 44 hits to go to reach that objective. "Nothing that ever happened to me before will equal the moment I make that hit. I won't be able to relax until I do."

There was ample reason for Musial to feel so deeply, so emotionally, about this particular baseball mark. And one anecdote, more than any other, probably points up the intensity of Stan's feeling.

Al Simmons, one of the genuinely outstanding hitters of the American League in the 1920s and early 1930s, played through 21 summers of baseball, in both leagues. Near the end of his career, in 1940 and 1941, when he returned to the Philadelphia Athletics, where he had experienced his finest years under Connie Mack, Simmons realized he was so terribly close to the goal of 3,000 hits. First he needed less than 200 hits to make it, then less than 100, then 73. But at that plateau he realized he could go no further towards his precious objective.

"When I was a young kid in this game," wailed Al Simmons, "I wasn't too eager to get in there every day. If I could stay out of the lineup by some excuse or other I did it. Sometimes I even played sick so Mr. Mack might pull me out of a game.

"But when I needed those few hits — 73 of them — I just couldn't get them. I was so near, yet so far. The time to get base hits is when you're young. I didn't take advantage of all of my opportunities, and now I can only blame myself for missing out on it."

Although he was elected to the Hall of Fame before he died, Simmons was bitter about his failure to reach 3,000 hits during his long playing span. But he was in good company. Some of the most prolific hitters in the game's history haven't been able to do it. The list of "failures" is almost shocking.

It includes names like Babe Ruth — 127 hits shy of the mark; Rogers Hornsby, a wash-out by 70 hits, yet often considered the best right-handed batter in National League history; Frankie Frisch; Lou Gehrig; Bill Terry; Pie Traynor (one of Musial's boyhood heroes); Wee Willie Keeler and Jimmy Foxx. There are, of course, dozens of other great players, too numerous to list here, who never even came close.

The last ballplayer to enter the Three Thousand Hit Club had been Paul Glee "Big Poison" Waner, who, like Pie Traynor, had been one of Musial's early idols,

93

when he played for the Pittsburgh Pirates. Paul made it, however, as a member of the Boston Braves in June 1942.

Since nobody else had qualified in the years after that, up to 1958, the exclusive group of 3,000-hitters was still composed only of Waner and those other giants of the baseball world — Ty Cobb, Tris Speaker, Honus Wagner, Nap Lajoie, Eddie Collins, and Cap Anson.

Needless to say, only those players with complete dedication, desire and talent have made this productive fraternity. The Three Thousand Hit Club, an eight-man society (many close observers of the game feel that few other modern players rate a chance to enter its doors), has inducted no flukes, no one-year wonders. It takes year-in, year-out, honest-to-goodness, total effort. These, in every way, are the true immortals of baseball.

And Stan Musial is one of them.

There was the time, shortly before Stan got the hit that won him membership in the club, that several writers tried to convince Stan how high he rated in the annals of the sport.

"He's one of the all-time greats even now," said one writer, "but he is hardly aware of it."

At the moment Stan was enjoying a little pre-game pepper session with some of his teammates. If he was one of the greats of the sport he was certainly still able to have fun in his profession. And the writers couldn't help but notice this aspect of his personality.

"Call him over," suggested Al Abrams of the Pittsburgh *Post-Gazette,* "and ask him if he realizes how close he is to some of the greatest players of all time."

Stan dropped out of the pepper game, with more than a little reluctance, and ambled over to the writing group.

"Do you ever read the record books, Stan?" Abrams asked.

"No," Stan answered. "What's the catch?"

"No catch at all," said Abrams. "It's just that the record book has a set of figures that puts you right up there with big shots like Ty Cobb and old Honus Wagner, who used to be a pretty well-known guy in Pittsburgh."

Stan was almost embarrassed by the praise. He drew his spikes through the dirt in front of the Card dugout and kept staring at the ground, as he answered Al Abrams.

"Gee, I'm really not that good," he said. "I can't be. But thanks."

As the 1958 season went winging into the middle of May, Stan's bat was hotter than a St. Louis hotel lobby (pre-air conditioning days, of course). He beat a tattoo on the pitches of all comers, and, as he approached a day game against the Chicago Cubs at Wrigley Field, on May 13, the game's mathematicians toted up his figures as 42 hits in the first 22 games.

After he banged out the 2,999th base hit of his life,

on Monday, May 12, Musial fully expected that he would remain out of the Cardinal lineup the next day in Chicago because Fred Hutchinson, dour-faced manager of the Cards, proved to have a sentimental streak in his nature.

"I'd like to have Stan get that 3,000th hit in front of a home town crowd in St. Louis," Hutchinson told the press. That meant that Stan would probably try for it on Wednesday, May 14, in St. Louis.

However, Hutchinson was taken to task by some observers, as well as a host of more pragmatic Card fans, for holding out his biggest weapon at the very time that the club was battling to get into contention in the pennant race.

As far as Stan was personally concerned, he would have liked to reserve the 3,000th blow for the home town folks. But whenever Hutch called on him, whether it was in Chicago or not, he was ready. He was anxious to annex that next hit and even if it were on Mars, he wanted it. He could taste it.

"I hope we win tomorrow against the Cubs," said Stan to Terry Moore, one of the Card coaches. "But if I walk four times I could save up that big hit for St. Louis. That's where I want to get into the club."

"I'd like to see you do it in St. Louis, too," said Terry. "So would Hutch."

The afternoon that Stan got into the club was delightful and sunny. He was down in the lobby of the

Knickerbocker Hotel in Chicago a little before noon, looking trim as ever in a black silk suit. He was well rested, even though he'd been up till almost three in the morning. Bill Heinz, a former newspaperman, who had been assigned the detail of "trailing Musial around" on this epochal day for a national magazine, found out the reason that Stan had been up that late on such an important occasion.

It seems that Stan's good friends, the Pizzicas, from Donora, had come in to Chicago to sweat out the 3,000th hit with him. During the course of the evening Molly Pizzica went to the wrong room in the hotel, and Stan spent several hours searching for her. He went into three theatres and walked up and down the aisles, peering into the seats. The police were called out to look for Molly, too. And hospitals were checked. It wasn't until nine o'clock on Tuesday morning that Molly called from her wrong room.

"It's funny now," said Lil Musial.

"But we were really worried," said Stan.

By noon Stan was on his way to the ball park, with the help of the Knickerbocker's doorman, who called a cab.

"Where to, mister?" said the driver.

"The old apple orchard," said Stan, with the eagerness of a fresh-faced rookie. "The old ball yard."

The driver didn't seem to get it.

"Wrigley Field," Stan said, understanding.

In the cab Musial politely answered Bill Heinz' questions. He is a humble man. But he has an appreciation of his increasing role as a baseball ambassador. He is, as the journalists often phrase it, good "copy," even if he lacks the obvious color of a Pepper Martin or a Bo Belinsky. He knew, too, that when he arrived at the Chicago ball park he would be subjected to an additional barrage of questions — unceasing questions and the unending demands of photographers, who never quite seemed to get just the "right" picture or just the "right" pose.

This is the kind of psychological pressure that has played havoc with the nerve endings of more than a single ballplayer in the past. Witness, for example, what it did to a man like Roger Maris, who, suddenly in 1961, found that his every word and action, both off and on the field, became public property. Many are convinced that Maris' unceasing petulance and frequent rudeness were due primarily to the fact that he was an unwilling victim of prodding and prying by the press. He could neither accept it nor cope with it in good humor.

Musial, on the other hand, has always been able to take the press in stride. He may, in his heart, be offended by some questions. But he never lets on. He may also be highly desirous of more privacy than they have been willing to grant him. But he refuses to get upset by it. He knows, as a reasonable man, that he isn't being persecuted or harassed, as Maris sometimes began to think, as he chased the ghost of Babe Ruth in '61. As modest as he is, Stan has always been able to appreciate, at least in more recent years, that he is a hero, an idol to millions of youngsters throughout this country. Therefore, he well knows that his actions and words, even his advice and opinions, are eagerly sought by all writers and newspapermen trying to perform their jobs.

That day in Chicago, as the photographers snapped pictures of him in every conceivable situation, prior to an event that everyone anticipated, he was cheery and good-humored. It didn't derail his equilibrium. It wasn't too much for a cooperative subject like Stan Musial. But it might have been too much for one of the photographers.

"I'm for letting up on the guy," said a photographer, who was part of the mob scene in the Card dressing room. "I think he's had enough of this stuff. Thanks, Stan."

Stan just looked at him and smiled.

"That's okay," he said.

As Manager Hutchinson had promised, Stan was not in the starting lineup for St. Louis. Hutch had gone on record as saying he wanted Stan "to save the big 3,000th hit for the home folks" and he was following through on his word.

Before the game Stan trotted slowly out to the Card bull pen, where he had decided he'd sun himself through a lazy afternoon. But as he sat there and watched the proceedings, the urge to join the action was strong in his mind. For one, by the beginning of the sixth inning his team had fallen behind by 3–1. And also, of course, he was terribly eager to have that 3,000th hit behind him. The most unlikely way to accomplish it was by baking his face in the Wrigley Field bull pen.

In the Card sixth Gene Green reached second base, with one out. Sam Jones, the Card pitcher, was scheduled to bat next. This was a situation that called for a pinch hitter. And in Manager Fred Hutchinson's mind that pinch hitter had to be Musial, even if he was going back on his promise to the fans of St. Louis to hold Stan out until the team returned to town.

So it was then that Hutch gestured to Coach Al Hollingsworth in the Card bull pen.

"Hey, Stan," the coach said. "Hutch wants you in there to bat."

Stan didn't have to be told twice, and neither did the fellow who handled the public address system.

"Now batting for Jones," came the announcement, "number six, Stan Musial."

There was a smallish crowd at hand in the park — perhaps 6,000 — (there might have been many more if Hutchinson hadn't made his pre-game statement about Stan not playing that day) but they started to applaud and shout and cheer, even as they recognized

Stan's figure coming towards the dugout to select his weapon of execution.

As Stan approached the plate, the shouting swelled into a roar. And when Stan casually squirmed into his place and stared coldly back over his right shoulder at Moe Drabowsky, the Chicago hurler, the roar became a command. These were, you must realize, almost all Cub partisans. But here they were now, begging this batter to get a hit. For the moment they could hardly have cared less about the result of the ball game.

What they wanted, what they could sense, what they could taste, was that 3,000th hit.

Now Stan was cobra-coiled into baseball's most familiar batting stance. First Drabowsky threw one wide for a ball. On the next two pitches Stan was cutting. But they both went foul. Then a ball swept low, making the count two and two. At two and two Stan connected with the next pitch solidly, but it was a long, loud foul into the left-field seats.

The crowd was impatient and imploring. They were also somewhat worried. But they shouldn't have been, for Stan, like most of the great hitters of all time, is a splendid batsman when two strikes have been charged against him.

Drabowsky then reared back and let fly. It was the pitch that was to make him a "reverse English" immortal. Stan liked what he saw and swung. The ball

Wide World Photos

Number 3,000.

headed in the direction of left field, where Cub outfielder Walt Moryn was stationed. But Walt hadn't the slightest chance of getting it. It bounced along the foul line and before Moryn could retrieve it Musial was perched safely on second base, with a typical Musial two-base hit.

But more important — Stan had his 3,000th hit!

Standing out there at second base, with a grin splitting his face, Stan received the plaudits of the crowd. Time was called and umpire Frank Dascoli, who had dutifully chased down the historic ball that Stan had just walloped, handed the pellet to Stan. There were now more photographers on the field than ballplayers and they insisted that Hutch should get into their pictures, pumping The Man's hand. Hutch was only too happy to oblige.

When Stan then came out of the ball game, to permit a pinch runner to take over his duties on the base paths, the crowd yelled and screamed its final appreciation. But nobody was applauding more than a blonde named Lil Musial, who occupied a front box that day close to the Card dugout.

Before disappearing into the Cardinal dugout, Stan went over to Lil and, like a husband returning from the office after a tough day, planted a tender kiss on her cheek.

When he was in the clubhouse, followed, of course, by the ubiquitous press, a photographer, who couldn't restrain his curiosity, asked Stan:

"Did you know that lady that you kissed out there?"

"I'd better," said Stan, throwing back his head and laughing, along with everbody else who heard the query. "That's my wife!"

Now, over and over again, came the questions. Most of them repeated the same refrain. What kind of pitch did you hit? How does it feel to have 3,000 hits in the bag? Do you think you'll be around long enough for 4,000?

Patiently, Stan fielded all of the questions, and posed for more pictures. How many times can a man grin in one day? How many times can he hold up "the ball" that he hit for his 3,000th? How many times can he shake Manager Hutchinson's calloused hand? How many times can he point to the exact spot on his bat where he connected for his big hit?

Well, if you're one of eight men out of some 11,000 major league ballplayers who have managed to reach the 3,000 summit, and if you happen to be the placid and imperturbable Stan Musial — you take it all in good spirit and come up for more.

Then, as Stan Musial did, you express true wonderment at the events of the day.

"You wouldn't think," he said, "that a little ball and a little bat could make such a big commotion!"

On a shelf near the showers, a radio kept blaring the details of the remainder of a Cub-Cards ball game that few, outside of Stan himself, seemed concerned about.

Stan interrupted one of his interrogators with a question. "How are we doing out there?"

"We got 'em, 5–3," answered Sam Jones, chewing on a toothpick.

"That's just great," said Stan, "we've got to win this one!"

A few more pictures, a few more questions.

"Yes, it feels just fine to make the 3,000th hit, just fine," said Stan, reacting as if he had never heard the question before.

Then the radio cut in: "The batter swings and misses. Strike three. The game's over. The Cards defeat the Cubs, 5–3."

Stan leaped to his feet.

"Hear that," he shouted, like a boy. "That makes it just perfect!"

That night, on the train taking the Cards and their national hero back to St. Louis, everyone was glowing with good feeling. Everyone felt as good about what had happened that afternoon at Wrigley Field as the fellow who had created all the fuss.

Stan was relaxing and laughing and swapping funny stories with his teammates and the writers.

"Did you know," chuckled Stan, "that when Hutch came out to shake my hand at second base today, he actually apologized to me. 'I'm sorry!' Hutch said to me. 'I know you wanted to wait to do it in St. Louis, but the club needed you today.'"

Bill Heinz, the reporter who was still carefully recording each detail of Musial's most memorable day in baseball, remembers that coach Terry Moore joined in the banter, too.

"Nobody will believe this," said Terry, "but once the smart guy pitchers walked me to get to this guy." Stan laughed as hard at the crack as anyone else.

After Stan finished his dinner in the diner, the train slowed down to make a stop.

What happened next, and for the rest of that exciting night, could only happen in America.

Word had, of course, seeped down to the tiniest hamlet in this Midwest area that Stan Musial, the man who only that day had knocked out the 3,000th hit of his career, was coming through by train. And what then could be more hospitable or more fitting than a group of "neighbors" to greet him at each stop along the way, like some conquering hero, or, better yet, like a Presidential candidate barnstorming for votes.

Some hardened reporters even likened Stan's reception that night to President Harry Truman's "whistle stop" successes of the 1948 Democratic campaign. "At every stop along the way," *The New York Times* veteran columnist Arthur Daley has written, "thousands of fans gathered to cheer . . . and Stan had to make speeches from the back platform . . ."

When the crowd that waited for Stan at Clinton, Illinois, began to chant "We want Musial, we want

Musial," Stan obliged by walking to the back platform. From there he could wave and smile and exchange small talk with the old folks and the youngsters who had ventured out into the night to greet a favorite person.

An hour later, when the train pulled into Springfield, more than 100 people were on hand. And all of them wanted either to shake Stan's hand or coax an autograph out of him. He satisfied all of them. Then he engaged in repartee with those nearest the platform.

"Did you all listen to that game today?" he asked.

"We sure did!" some of the crowd answered. Others simply shouted "Yes."

"We beat 'em, didn't we?" Stan shouted.

"Yes," they shouted back.

"Good," said Stan, punctuating his "address."

As the train pulled out of Springfield the crowd warmed up its own version of "For He's a Jolly Good Fellow," and Stan smiled. But there was a lump in his throat the size of that baseball he'd smacked a few hours earlier.

After all of the excitement and noise, Stan sat down in the parlor car, yawned as he spread-eagled his legs, and, almost in an instant, he was fast asleep.

It was well past midnight when the train chugged into the St. Louis station. But there were almost a thousand people waiting for him there. The people cheered him lustily and shook his hands and scrambled for his autograph, as photographers and police battled to get close enough to guard him or take his picture.

And all the while a little smile played across Stan's face.

He didn't say it in so many words, but anyone who knew Stan Musial at all, knew that he had to be thinking what a lucky guy he was. For Stan, ever the modest man, could never quite believe he was deserving of all this acclaim and adulation.

"You've got to be lucky," Stan keeps insisting. And that's the way he felt, in triplicate, the night he came home to St. Louis, the hero of the 3,000th hit.

CHAPTER TEN

HE'S ONLY HUMAN

Despite the fact that most pitchers wouldn't agree, Stan Musial is the first to confess that he is only human. He has had his slumps, unpredictable and vexing, and sometimes persistent. And he has had his bad days. And he has been fooled on occasion, and he has been off in his timing. But with it all, he is probably the greatest player of his time.

Even that notorious churl Ty Cobb, the only man who now rates as a more prolific batsman than Musial, was able, before he died, to put his wholehearted stamp of approval on Stan.

That is saying more than a mouthful, too. For praise from Cobb never came easy. He was obsessed with the notion that all old-timers could do it better than the moderns. He never ceased to rage at the way baseball is played today. He worshiped the past, as so many of us do in other activities and human endeavors. And he found little to appreciate on the contemporary scene.

That is, very little, except one Stan Musial.

"He's my kind of ballplayer," Cobb once wrote about Musial, in an article in which he assailed the weaknesses of most modern-day players.

"He has the power of Nap Lajoie, the stamina of Eddie Collins, and is as steady as Honus Wagner," added Cobb, in his paean to Stan. "No man has ever been a perfect ballplayer. But Musial comes closest to being the most perfect in the game today. I've seen great hitters and great runners and great fielders. But he puts them all together like no one else, except the way George Sisler did. He's certainly one of the greatest hitters of all time. In my book he's a better player than Joe DiMaggio was in his prime."

Coming from a man like Ty Cobb, this had to be the highest form of flattery.

But, when he was apprised of Cobb's remarks, beatifying him in Tyrus' personal Hall of Fame, Stan had very little to say. Only: "I don't want to argue with him. But I don't think there was a day I ever could reach DiMaggio."

Ty Cobb would have been the first man to admit,

too, that even the greats like Musial have to suffer slumps on occasion. Ty had them during his uproarious and fantastic diamond life. And the frustrating experiences of such wonderful batters as Ted Williams in the 1946 World Series, and Willie Mays at the very outset of his career with the Giants are only two instances of the inevitability of slumps, even for the top hitters.

Surprisingly, right after Stan's great 1946 season, when he led the Cards to a National League flag, and a world title, with a .365 batting average (which helped to win him the Most Valuable Player award), he had one of his most disastrous seasons. He managed finally to hit for a .312 average in 1947, but only after painstaking effort and a continual uphill struggle that started practically on opening day.

As the Cards started the season with only two victories in their first 13 games, Stan's average was below .200! By the middle of May, when such kinks are usually straightened out, Stan was barely hitting .140, and eyebrows were raised around the circuit. Had the league's pitchers found out how to slip fast balls or curves or knucklers past Stan's unorthodox crouch? What could possibly be wrong with him, coming off such a wonderful 1946 season?

As the slump plagued him, Stan sought a solution. But it wasn't to be found with his technique or his batting eye. It simply turned out that he was suffering from a badly inflamed appendix, which was, according to the doctors that Stan consulted, in need of immediate surgical attention.

In St. Louis, where Dr. Bob Hyland, one of baseball's most celebrated medical men, examined Stan's appendix, it was suggested that Musial take care of the problem at once. But Stan felt very strongly about staying in the lineup to help his team.

"Is there any way to postpone this operation until after the season?" Stan asked.

"Yes, we can freeze it," said Dr. Hyland.

And that's exactly what was done.

Stan, after a brief period of hospitalization, returned to the lineup. Slowly, but inexorably, his average began to move in the direction of respectability. With a big month of August, when he hit well over .400, Stan brought his average home over the .300 mark.

There is an amusing story connected with Stan's aggravated appendix and the subsequent slump. During the winter preceding the 1947 season, Stan had taken up golf seriously for the first time. Several of his best friends from Donora, including Andrew Sukel, who had been the principal of Donora High School when Stan was there, had urged him to play golf for relaxation and to stay in good shape.

"We played golf practically all that winter," recalls Mr. Sukel. "There was a group of us — Charlie Wunderlich, the basketball coach; Wendell Hallen, the bandmaster; myself and Stan. Stan worked at the grocery, too. But almost every spare moment he had he was on that course, our local Butler golf course.

"It was really amusing that Stan didn't play well at first. He was even reluctant to play golf, because he likes to excel at whatever he does. But finally he accepted it as a challenge and we all were delighted to see how well he was playing the game once he decided to commit himself to it.

"However, when the 1947 season began — and Stan was in such a dreadful slump at the plate — all of us who encouraged him to play golf, felt terribly guilty about what we thought was our part in this sad state of affairs. We were convinced that it was golf that put him in his slump and, what's more, we were willing to accept responsibility for what had happened to him.

"When we found out that it was the appendix that was bothering him — and not his golf — we were the most relieved fellows you've ever seen in your life."

For his part Stan never felt that his participation in off-season golf had affected his hitting eye one iota. If he had known of the secret guilt felt by his companions from Donora he would have been the first to alleviate them of their distress.

In Musial's book luck, pure and simple, plays a role in hitting. And if a fellow doesn't have any of that going for him, plus his natural talent, of course, he might as well hang up his spikes.

Once when Stan was sitting around in a bull session with a bunch of his friends and discussing the usual thing — you guessed it — his hitting, he said:

"I can feel a slump coming on in my bones. I'm getting too many lucky hits. I'm not smashing the ball the way I should. Soon my good luck will desert me."

As usual, in such matters, Stan was 100 percent accurate. Soon he found himself in a miserable slump. And soon after that, only his unusual talents as a hitter, and luck, combined again to restore his batting average and his batting eye.

In more recent years, naturally, when Stan's average slumped to non-Musial dimensions (which means below .300), part of the reason had to be his inability to beat out as many "leg" hits as he used to make in his halcyon days. In his younger days Stan was a deceptively fast man going down the line to first, or tearing into second on a two-bagger. Ted Williams, himself, once suggested that if he only had had Musial's speed of foot he could have added a dozen points to his average each year. When you're a young man, such fleet-footedness can help terminate many a slump. When you're in the twilight of your baseball life, dragging spikes can make you pay a heavy penalty — especially in terms of points on a batting average.

Stan's public over the years has been tolerant and understanding. When he has been bogged down in a slump, they have waited patiently for him to emerge. They have, on occasion, even cheered his efforts when he has popped up or grounded out. At the All-Star Game at Chicago's Wrigley Field in 1962, when Stan came to bat in the third inning, the ovation was positively deafening. Then, when he was thrown out at first base on a routine grounder to shortstop Luis Aparicio, the large crowd continued to cheer him. When he trotted out to left field, to replace Los Angeles' Tommy Davis, one of the stars of the future, the crowd roared again.

"It is like the crowd was saying 'This is worth the price of admission,'" wrote Ed Sinclair of the New York *Herald Tribune*.

Unfortunately, however, Stan has also suffered the slings and arrows of the embittered clientele. But never as much, and with as much ferocity, as other idols before him.

In 1956, during the September stretch drive, Stan had a particularly poor afternoon at Busch Stadium. Shifted to first base by Manager Fred Hutchinson, Stan made two glaring boots at the position. To make matters even more insufferable, he went hitless, as the Dodgers won, 5–3. The result of this performance was a rare panning by his home town audience. When Stan Musial is booed in St. Louis, that's news. And on this occasion, it was.

Hardened reporters were somewhat reluctant to query their friend on the subject. But they did get his views on another topic: a ballplayer's fatigue.

"It was easier to play ball in the old days, I guess," said Stan. "If we dropped a game then, it wasn't a matter to worry about, or to cause anybody to start pressing. We knew in the long run we were going to end up on top. We knew we had it. But times have changed." They certainly had when Stan Musial was being booed in Busch Stadium.

In 1959, a year in which Stan batted only .255, and got only 13 doubles (the all-time low of his baseball life), the rumor-mongers were hard at work dispossessing him of his job and his future. To set the record straight, he did look tired and his overall statistics showed it. There were many days that he sat out the second game of double-headers. Often, too, if an afternoon game followed a night game, he was permitted to remain on the bench for the day contest. This certainly was not the Musial of old, for Stan had been, next to Iron Man Lou Gehrig, one of the most durable ballplayers who ever lived.

However, there was no real provocation for his being booed in St. Louis. He had given too many years of effort and energy to deserve such unkindness. Yet, here he was, the recipient of an unexpected roasting from some unthinking Cardinal fans.

Then, one of the most unusual things in the history

of the game occurred. Many fans, who appreciated Stan's years of loyalty and devotion to the Card cause, retorted publicly to the heresy of booing their idol.

They paid for advertisements in the St. Louis papers and apologized to Stan for the boorishness and forgetfulness of others. While slapping down the cult of nonbelievers, they reminded Stan of their own continuing admiration.

Through all of these trying times, Stan reacted as he always has: he gentlemanly refused to comment about his critics, while feeling deeply grateful to those who had sought to upbraid his detractors.

However, the grumpy voices of his critics have been the exception to the rule. Stan continues to be the favorite of the fans, his fellow players, his foes, and even the umps, whether he's going good, bad — or simply isn't going.

Tributes to him keep coming from the most unlikely sources. Dusty Boggess, a hardened National League umpire with over two decades of calling 'em on his job record, says:

"Look, guys like Stan Musial never give you trouble. It's only the bushers."

Stan receives the same kind of support from the stands. Some years ago, when Stan was on one of his pleasant and productive visits to the Polo Grounds, he happened to be caught up in an inexplicable slump that had him tearing out his thinning hair. But the slump was working even greater hardships on those who rooted for the Cardinal.

There was one fan in particular, a robust fellow of Polish extraction who managed to attend almost every New York and Brooklyn game that Stan played in, who suffered the tortures of the damned as Stan's bat failed to speak. Each time the fan exhorted Stan to whack a homer or slash a double — or even hit a tiny single — Stan would have difficulty even connecting with the ball.

"Hit one for me, Stosh baby," the fan implored. And Stan struck out.

"Now's the one, Stosh boy," yelled the insistent loyalist. And Stan rolled out meekly to the second baseman.

The last time Stan came to bat the rooter just knew he couldn't fail again.

"I'm looking at that homer now, Stosh baby," he bellowed. And almost everybody in the park could hear it, including Stan.

Stan tried, as he always does, to come through for his anonymous but strident friend. But things weren't breaking his way and the best he could do was pop up to the first baseman.

Musial felt bad enough, as he trotted forlornly back to his post at first base. But that was nothing compared to the frustration and woe he had brought upon the head of his one-man fan club. But did the stricken fan turn on his idol?

He most certainly did not. Instead, as Stan's head remained bowed at first base, almost in expectation of a mighty raspberry from the stands, the fan held out his own special brand of reassurance. Everyone in hearing range of Coogan's Bluff could hear it, too.

"Don't worry, Stosh honey baby," he roared, a tear in his voice, "those monkeys can't shine your shoes."

One recalls that nobody in the vicinity disagreed with him.

Although Stan's hitting was instrumental in landing the Cards in four World Series — 1942, 1943, 1944 and 1946 — he did not sparkle in any of them. He owns a single World Series home run, a blow he hit in the fourth game of the 1944 Series off Sig Jakucki of the St. Louis Browns. In only one World Series has Stan hit as high as .300. That was in 1944 when he batted .304 and made seven hits in a six-game Series. In both 1942 and 1946 he hit a depressingly low .222, hardly a fetching figure for an immortal.

In 1946, when the World Series clash between the Cards and the Boston Red Sox was billed as a showdown between the two greatest batters in baseball — Stan for the Redbirds and Ted Williams for the Red Sox — both men developed a strange case of the blind staggers throughout the nip-and-tuck seven games. Williams managed to connect for only five measly singles, for a .200 average, and one run batted in. Stan, on the other hand, had six hits, just one more than Ted, for his .222 mark. But four of his safeties were doubles, while one was a triple. In addition, Musial batted in four runs.

If anyone was returned the victor in that contest of baseball titans, it had to be Musial. But it wasn't the kind of performance that could have satisfied Stan, any more than it did the tempest-tossed Williams.

Even if Stan's World Series record has left something to be desired, Tom Meany, the veteran baseball writer, once insisted in a story on Musial that he "never has really had a bad Series." Meany was assessing Stan on his overall play, for too many observers have neglected to consider Stan's defensive skill. Whether he has played in the outfield or at first base he has always been capable of turning in a first-rate job.

Before Stan met Ted Williams head-on in the 1946 Series, the one that Country Slaughter swiped from under Boston's nose by his seventh-game baserunning, Leo Durocher had commented about the two men's capabilities. There was little doubt that he was awfully high on Stan.

"I don't see much of Williams," said Durocher, "but they tell me he's a great hitter. But nobody compares him with this guy Musial, as a ballplayer, do they? This fellow is a great hitter. He can run and field and throw and slide. He can play anywhere in the outfield for you or come in and play first base. And don't forget he used to pitch. I guess he'd catch if you asked him to."

If Stan didn't quite live up to Leo's advance billing in the 1946 World Series, it was probably partially attributable to the fact that baseball, like any competitive game, has a certain element of luck in it. This is easily borne out by the fact that it has almost become axiomatic and traditional at World Series time for the unsung, hummingbird hitters to distinguish themselves, while the acknowledged sluggers go begging for base hits.

Wasn't there a World Series in which Gil Hodges played through seven complete games without getting a single hit? And haven't relatively anonymous types like Pepper Martin, Billy Werber, Gene Woodling, Billy Martin, Bobby Richardson, Al Gionfriddo, Chuck Hiller and Johnny Edwards suddenly come alive, with feats of hitting and fielding that have made them look like supermen?

Stan, the year-in, year-out superman of the Cards, has never quite made the black headlines for his Series play.

In 1942, when the Cards smashed the Yankees into pieces with a victory in five games after they had dropped the opener, the special St. Louis heroes were third baseman Whitey Kurowski and pitchers Johnny Beazley and Ernie White. Stan went hitless in the first and last games. In between, however, he got himself four hits and robbed Joe Gordon of a home run with a spectacular catch close to the box seats in left field.

The next year, 1943, as the Yankees gained revenge with a five-game triumph over the Cards, Stan hit in every game but the last. However, while batting .278, he had no extra base hits and no runs batted in. For Cardinal honors he had to take a back seat to shortstop Marty Marion, who batted .357 from his eighth-place perch in the St. Louis batting order.

As the Cards won a mid-war third consecutive National League flag in 1944, the St. Louis Browns, their home town rival, were the American League representatives.

The Cards had little difficulty deflating the Brownies, who had won their first American League pennant in history. It was in the fourth game of this Series that Stan, for the first and only time in his experience, banged out three hits in a World Series contest.

Red Smith, the famous syndicated sports columnist, once commented about Stan that the "only sure way to get him out was to get him out of town." As you can see, this pun never aptly applied to Musial at World Series time. But any other time of day or night, Red Smith knew what he was writing about. No National League hitter of modern times has been more feared or more respected.

CHAPTER ELEVEN

THAT WONDERFUL GUY

Americans are often inclined to exaggerate the virtues of their heroes. Often, when a "hero" has faded into the shadows after being in the limelight, his true personality or private image is then revealed, bit by bit, to the public. Is this, then, to be the case with Stan The Man? Is his real personality just a pale imitation of what he is cracked up to be? Is he, like so many athletes and movie stars and politicians, simply the end product of excessive press agentry?

Has Stan The Man been eulogized in the press miles beyond justification? Does he really warrant the unstinted, flowery praise he has always received? Does he really radiate good will, unlimited charm and gentle-

123

ness? Is he the living embodiment of all the major virtues?

Is he unfailingly courteous, kind, obedient, gracious, decent, helpful, humble, truthful? Is he the manager's ideal, as Fred Hutchinson once suggested? ("You don't manage him at all," said Hutchinson, when he piloted the Cards. "He manages himself.")

Is he really the ideal of contemporary sports heroes, a man who would never aspire to undermine a man he works for, or a manager he plays under?

Some years ago, when Stan's name was occasionally mentioned as a managerial possibility for the Cardinals, he issued a statement on his attitude about managers. It could well be adopted as a code by all major league players. "Any man I play for, I got to think he's the best in the business," said Musial. "I like to play my game. I don't like to worry about everything else. So all the guys I've played for, I got to think each one of them was the best."

Is Stan then, in a sense — and this is not meant as a criticism or as a cynical judgment — a classic boy scout? The answer is simply — *yes*.

There is possibly no better place to go for corroboration of this estimate than to some of those men who have played alongside Stan in recent years. If this is a thoughtful soul who never misses a Sunday in church or never forgets to send Christmas cards to his old friends, this is also a man who demands of others the ultimate in team effort and spirit.

For instance, at spring training in St. Petersburg, Florida, not too long ago, one of the younger Cardinals went into second base on a close play, standing up. When the boy came running off the diamond, Stan trotted alongside of him and, looking him squarely in the eye, said in a soft but persuasive manner:

"When you play on this club you *slide,* even when it's spring training."

Kenny Boyer, a fine all-around third baseman, who is also the captain of the Cards, says that Musial is "great with kids."

"He's not a rah-rah guy," says Boyer. "He's good-natured and likes to rib and be ribbed. But it's not in what he says or does that he's an inspiration. It's really the character of the man that counts. He's living proof that nice guys don't have to finish last."

Over the long grind of years in baseball, with Stan's increased stature as a star and his evolution from small-town boy to $100,000-a-year man with diverse investments, has he changed? Has he become aloof or petulant or wary of the press and public? Not in the least, according to Red Schoendienst, the freckle-faced old pro, who has known The Man as roommate, fellow player and intimate pal for some 16 years.

"The only way I can think that Stan has changed,"

grins Red, "is that now he's hitting the ball harder."

Carl Warwick, a former Texas Christian University student who started the 1962 season with the Cards before being traded to Houston, discussed Stan's help in glowing terms.

"Any time anyone asks me a question about Stan I'm glad to answer," said twenty-five-year-old Carl. "He's always quiet until someone — maybe one of the rookies like myself — puts a question to him. Then he can't do enough for you. He's very patient and kind. You'd never know for a moment that his name is Stan Musial, because he never tries to run the show. I've talked to him a great deal about hitting and about my batting stance. There's one thing he'll never do: try to teach you his own batting stance. That's out. He'll just help you with your own stance. He'll watch you carefully during a game, then come to you with suggestions."

Another Card youngster, Doug Clemens, a twenty-three-year-old outfielder from Leesport, Pennsylvania, has had the same experience with Stan.

"He's always around to help," said Doug. "He's one of the most cooperative men I've ever met when it comes to giving advice."

There was a time when Chuck Connors, the TV star of Rifleman fame, carried a first baseman's mitt, instead of a more lethal stage weapon. Chuck once served a brief apprenticeship with the Brooklyn Dodgers in 1949 and the Chicago Cubs in 1951. In those days he had a strong desire to survive in the majors, despite his limited talent.

Frustrated by major league pitching, Chuck sought to iron out the flaws in his batting style. First he discussed it with his Cub teammates.

"There's only one guy to go to," they said, "that's Musial. He'll help you, if he can."

When the Cards came into Chicago, Connors, who couldn't help feeling he was imposing on Stan, finally introduced himself to Musial. With that barrier out of the way, he asked Stan if he'd take a few seconds off to watch him hit in batting practice.

"I'd be glad to," said Stan.

After Stan leaned against the batting cage and gave Chuck's efforts his keen once-over, he took the rookie aside and chatted about the finer points of hitting for fifteen minutes.

"I was a bum of a hitter, just not cut out for the majors," recalls Connors, who has made it big in another profession. "But I will never forget Stan's kindness. When he was finished watching me cut away at the ball, Stan slapped me on the back and told me to keep swinging."

Stan's innate decency and respect for others is something that Bill White, the hard-hitting Cardinal first baseman, is also quite willing to pinpoint in his appraisal of the man. White happens to be a Negro — and is a most articulate one. He has a keen appreciation of the social struggle that has taken place in baseball, ever since the eventful day that Jackie Robinson first joined the Brooklyn Dodgers in the mid-1940s.

"Sure, I've asked Stan questions about batting," said White. "He's helpful to anyone who asks him. But more important, I guess, is his cooperative, pleasant attitude towards *anyone* — white or black — who approaches him. It doesn't make any difference to him. He's that kind of man.

"In baseball, you know, a man makes few friends. You make buddies. I'd guess you'd call my relationship with Stan a 'buddy' relationship. But he's always congenial. You can kid with him, or get advice."

Musial is not a professional crusader for civil rights, nor is he a special pleader for minorities. Yet he has shown a sensitiveness about treating all people with respect.

The story is told of how Stan once shared a cab in New York with several of his teammates. The driver of the cab, according to the license card that was available to the view of the ballplayers, was a man with a name that provoked tasteless mimicry on the part of one of Stan's mates. The player should have known better, but he didn't. If someone had accused him of being anti-Semitic, he probably would have heatedly denied it. But still he persisted in his little joke, gesticulating and talking in a harsh Yiddish accent.

Finally, Stan, who was made uncomfortable and

embarrassed by his teammate's rudeness, spoke up.

"That's enough of that stuff," he said, sharply. "Knock it off now. We've heard enough of it."

As soon as Stan registered his feelings about his unthinking teammate's behavior in the cab, the abuse stopped as promptly as it had started. Then an icy calm prevailed in the cab until the driver pulled his car up to the Polo Grounds.

Thinking he could make amends for his obnoxious behavior, the Cardinal then handed a bill to the taxi driver as he was about to hop out of the cab.

But Stan quickly shoved his arm and the money away. "No, I'll take it," he said.

When the cab had pulled away, Stan tried to make it quite clear, once and for all, how he felt about what had just gone on in his presence.

Turning to the guilty party, he said:

"Do me a favor, will you please, and don't bother to ride with me again."

Perhaps Stan didn't mean to be the champion of an often oppressed and beleaguered minority group. But still he had acted with his best instincts. That is the kind of a man he is — at all times.

If Stan has always shown great respect and courtesy towards those less fortunate than himself, he has also demonstrated his great concern for children, other people's and his own.

In 1946 Bernardo Pasquel, a peso-packing Mexican

who had a desire to create a baseball empire south of the border by luring some of the best American talent into his country, made sounds in Musial's direction. Stan had batted .357 in 1943, to lead the National League for his first time, and .347 in 1944. He'd been in military service in 1945.

If Pasquel had been able to land Stan he would have had for himself one of the biggest fish in the pond. He had already enticed Cardinals like Max Lanier, Fred Martin and Lou Klein to join his operation in Mexico, and pitcher Sal Maglie, a Giant property, also had cast his lot with him.

At the time Musial was in the $15,000 class as a ballplayer. Pasquel snorted at such a salary.

"I can make you rich, amigo," promised Pasquel, who was thoroughly familiar with the reputation that Card president Sam Breadon had in money matters. In some quarters in baseball Breadon was considered to be a twentieth-century version of Scrooge.

Stan's susceptibility to Pasquel's offer was increased by the fact that his family had grown to three now — two boys and a girl — and because he had just rented a bungalow for the summer in a fairly high rent district of St. Louis. If ever a man was primed to snap up the kind of big money that Pasquel and his brother Jorge were flashing, it was the up-and-coming star of baseball, Stan Musial.

First Bernardo Pasquel threw $75,000 in cash onto Musial's well-scrubbed kitchen table.

"Sign on the dotted line," said Pasquel, "and you'll have $125,000 more for five years of playing."

Musial's face flushed with excitement. This was really a tremendous amount of money that this man was offering him. It could set him up for life. He would never, he thought, be able to make this kind of money with St. Louis.

"I'd like to have more time to think about your generous offer," said Stan. He had discouraged the Pasquel brothers once before when they had tried to sign him. But they were unwilling to take no for an answer. Now, despite his hesitation, they thought they had him at last.

The next day, troubled and impatient to make a decision in the matter, Stan went to Manager Eddie Dyer for advice.

"What should I do, Eddie?" asked Stan. "That's an awful lot of money they're offering."

Musial had always had a great deal of fondness and respect for Dyer. He was perfectly willing to listen to Dyer, as he had listened to Billy Southworth, and later as he would listen to Fred Hutchinson.

Dyer spoke from the heart to Stan. Perhaps he also spoke with the best interests of the Cards in mind. But Stan didn't think he was being deceitful or misleading.

131

"If you leave the Cards and accept this money from the Mexican league," began Eddie, "you will, as you well know, be breaking off your contract with the Cards. You'll be walking away from the majors for good. They'll probably never let you back in." Then he paused a second.

"But more than that, Stan," continued Dyer, almost in a paternal manner, "you might conceivably be causing your kids embarrassment in school as they grow up. I can just hear some people pointing to your children and saying, 'There go the kids of a fellow whose word was no darned good.'"

The Pasquels were eager to get Stan's final decision on their offer. So they met with him again a few days later.

"What have you decided to do?" asked Bernardo.

"I've decided to stay where I am," said Stan quietly. "I couldn't bear hurting my kids. And if I broke my contract with the Cards that's what I'd be doing."

With that declaration he said "Gracias" and good-by to the men who were smart enough to try to cajole the greatest star in the game.

Stan had echoed Dyer's advice. But that's why he had gone to him in the first place.

He never regretted turning down the Mexicans. But the Pasquels regretted it. The addition of such a player to their setup might have made their dream of an empire come true.

A little boy named Hal Breitinberg, who lives in Springfield, Virginia, could also testify to the thoughtfulness of Stan The Man.

In 1960 Hal's daddy, Eugene Breitinberg, a captain in the Army, was stationed in Korea. The captain had been a long-time baseball fan and an admirer of Stan.

One day he picked up a copy of an old magazine which had a funny picture of Stan in it. In the picture Stan was surrounded by eight small cardinal birds. At the time Captain Breitinberg's outfit had a rather talented Korean refugee artist attached to it, and it struck the captain that it would be a nice idea to have Stan's picture reproduced by this fellow. After the artist completed his work, it was taken back to the United States by Captain Breitinberg and immediately tacked onto six-year-old Hal's wall. It remained there for young Hal to admire, until one day Captain Breitinberg realized Stan himself was in Washington, D. C., for an All-Star baseball game.

Captain Breitinberg thought it would be fun to call Stan and tell him about the painting.

"So I phoned him," recalls the captain, "to tell him, not only about the art work that hung on my boy's wall, but also about my great admiration for him.

"Mrs. Musial answered the phone, and after asking my name, put Stan on. I told him my story and that I had always hoped some day to have the honor of taking a picture of him with my son Hal.

"Right away Stan asked us both to come over to the ball park before the game and to ask the groundkeeper to take us to him. This we did and Stan obliged us by posing for the nicest picture with Hal.

"Although he is one of the greatest players in the history of baseball Stan's modesty was such that I became almost ashamed of my own forwardness. He left an impression on my son that I know will last through his life . . . his simple kindness toward two strangers seemed to me the greatest play of the day . . ."

CHAPTER TWELVE

A NIGHT FOR STAN

Stan The Man has always occupied a special niche in the minds and hearts of everybody — players, press, fans, and even umpires.

Some years ago, as the story goes, a rookie pitcher was facing Stan in a critical moment of a ball game. The rookie wound up and threw a pitch that was as close to the strike zone as you can get without chalking up a strike. The umpire called it a ball. And the pitcher howled like a tortured banshee.

"If that wasn't a strike, I'll eat it," screamed the hurler.

"Young fellow," responded the umpire, "Mr. Musial will be delighted to let you know when you pitch a strike."

One of Stan's proudest moments was when he met President John F. Kennedy the day after the All-Star Game of July 10, 1962. The President presented Musial with an autographed photograph.

Stan has been accorded this kind of respect for years. And more likely than not it comes from the opposition, too.

In 1962, for example, the New York Mets were a party to something almost unique in baseball annals: they set aside a special night for Stan, on August 18, and presented him with a pile of gifts, including a radio, a shotgun, a fishing rod (from a fair country hitter by the name of Ted Williams), sport shirts, a year's supply of coffee and, most important of all, a scholarship fund set up in his name at Columbia College in New York City.

Now it is nothing unusual for a ballplayer as venerable and as distinguished in his trade as Stan to be honored by his own home town fans. One of the most commendable traits of most baseball fans is that they dearly love the home town team and the home town players, come what may. There have been notable exceptions to this rule, of course. But it is certainly a rarity when a low-down "foreigner" from another ball club gets more applause than the local hero. What made Stan Musial Night at the Polo Grounds so incredible was that the enemy — in this case the New York Mets — was paying homage to a man who in other years had done everything he could to destroy the New York Giants in this very ball park. And now he was about to make the same effort against Casey Stengel's newly minted and highly inept athletes.

In a sense, the fact that the Mets were paying tribute

to an out-of-town player was only a natural extension of the high regard that Mr. Stengel of the Mets has always had for Stan. He has, on more than a single occasion, confessed almost a small boy's idolatry of the Cardinal star.

"Stan is a tremendous figure," old Casey said in 1962. "He gets along with everybody. He never tried to show up an umpire and is never boastful. He's a hero to me, too."

Stan has never wowed anyone with his flow of oratory. He is certainly not the world's best after-dinner speaker. And before dinner he doesn't rival Bob Hope or Milton Berle, either. But if there is one image he projects, as he nervously clutches a microphone, it is of a man consumed by modesty and humility. Stan *is* sincere.

Fighting to hold back the tears, Stan first thanked his Cardinal teammates for helping to make this night possible. (Wasn't it Yogi Berra who, in a similar situation, malapropped: "I'd like to thank my Yankee teammates for making this night necessary.")

Then Stan said: "I especially want to thank the Mets for bringing National League baseball back to New York so that I could play here once more."

From the start of his little speech the crowd of 15,000 fans warmed to Musial. But it was only when Stan had finished — "Thanks from the bottom of my heart . . . words just can't express how I feel" — that they really let him know how they felt. They clapped and whistled and yelled and stamped. If you didn't know he was a boy from Donora, you might have thought he was a product of the sidewalks of New York. In the past only immortals like Babe Ruth, Lou Gehrig, Willie Mays and Mel Ott had earned this kind of reception from a New York audience.

A huge plaque presented to Stan on his night featured this inscription:

THE NEW YORK FANS, THROUGH THE METS, SALUTE THE GREATEST BALLPLAYER OF HIS GENERATION FOR OVER TWO DECADES. STAN MUSIAL OF THE ST. LOUIS CARDINALS HAS ENHANCED THE PRESTIGE OF THE NATIONAL LEAGUE BOTH ON AND OFF THE FIELD.

Stan could be proud, too, that the man in America's White House, John Fitzgerald Kennedy, had not forgotten him on his big night in New York. As he read the telegram that President Kennedy had sent to him, Stan's eyes glowed.

CONGRATULATIONS ON TWO DECADES OF ACHIEVEMENTS IN THE MAJOR LEAGUES. IN 1942 YOU BATTED .315, AND NOW 20 YEARS LATER, YOU ARE BATTING .339. YOU MAKE US ALL BELIEVE THAT LIFE REALLY BEGINS AT 40. WITH WARM REGARDS, JOHN F. KENNEDY.

During the heated 1960 Presidential campaign between Mr. Kennedy and Richard M. Nixon of California, the Republican candidate, Stan had publicly supported and campaigned for Mr. Kennedy. It was during those busy days that the future President had quipped, when he was informed of Stan's political position: "They say you're too old to play baseball and I'm too young to be President. We ought to get together."

The Stan Musial Scholarship at Columbia, however, was probably the most enduring thrill that came Stan's way that night. Though Stan had originally bypassed college because of his desire to play baseball, he is aware of the importance of higher education for youngsters in America.

"If I had to do it all over again," said Stan before the ceremonies of the evening, "I would have accepted a basketball scholarship before going into baseball. There's no telling how far a man can go with a college education."

Then Stan tried to explain to all of his admirers why he was so delighted that Columbia, which had sent those great major leaguers Eddie Collins and Lou Gehrig on their way to fame, was the college that had been picked for the Musial Scholarship.

"It's denominational — that's why I'm glad it was Columbia," said Stan. "Tell me, is that the right word?"

When it was pointed out to Stan that he meant to say that Columbia was non-denominational, he laughed and then said, half-seriously:

"If I had gone to college on that basketball scholarship, I would have had that word right, wouldn't I?"

There was a ball game on Stan Musial Night, too. But since Stan had played against a right-handed Mets

Wide World Photos

Casey Stengel bows in homage to Stan at the beginning of "Stan Musial Night" in the Polo Grounds on August 18, 1962.

pitcher in the day game, Manager Johnny Keane decided to leave the guest of honor on the sidelines for the evening. The fans, however, would have no part of that arrangement. As soon as the Cardinal lineup came crackling over the loudspeaker system, they realized Keane intended to rest Stan for the night. From the first inning on they set up a steady chant, asking for Stan's presence in the ball game.

"We want Musial. We want Stan!" they implored. Finally, when the Cards were ahead, 8–0, Stan was

141

called off the bench to pinch hit. They cheered when he picked up his bat and when he took his position at the plate. When he drew a walk, he was cheered mightily as he trotted slowly down to first.

Then, when Manager Keane sent in a runner for Stan, the park again shook with cheers — mind you, for an enemy ballplayer who had done nothing but garner a base on balls and then departed from the premises.

"They'd cheer this guy even for lacing up his shoes," declared one observer who was on hand for Stan Musial Night.

At a party later that night at Toots Shor's, the rotund restaurateur, who has seen plenty of great ballplayers during the years he has catered to the appetites of many illustrious New Yorkers, took advantage of the occasion to pronounce that Stan "is the greatest ballplayer that ever lived, with the exception of Babe Ruth."

Toots Shor was merely echoing what every sane baseball follower has been saying about Stan for years. After Frank Lane had been general manager of the Cards for only two years he was moved to say:

"Stan is the only ballplayer I've ever met who would get me to stand in line for his autograph."

"You mean an autograph on the bottom of a contract, don't you?" asked a bystander.

"Certainly not," said Lane. "I mean his autograph on the bottom of a scorecard."

CHAPTER THIRTEEN

THE HOMER HE
COULDN'T HIT

Before Horace Stoneham plucked his New York Giants out of the Polo Grounds and set them down in a San Francisco wind tunnel, Willie Mays used to play some of his best ball in the steaming, garbage-cluttered streets of Harlem. Willie may have been one of the world's greatest and highest-priced ballplayers, but he still loved to play stickball with the Negro youngsters. These kids had a special spot in their hearts for Willie and he returned the feeling.

One of the few other ballplayers alive today who would still play the game for nothing — as Willie did — is Stan Musial.

What does Stan often do on his day off?
He plays ball, of course.
Who does he play with?
With the kids. Who else?

"He'll even get on a baseball diamond with his daughters [Jeanne and Janet]," says Mrs. Musial. "When the Sacred Heart Academy used to have a mother-daughter field day, who do you think umpired the softball game? My husband."

Stan loves to tell jokes and do magic tricks with cards. He loves to take pictures of his children and tickle the keys of a piano. He delights in talking about baseball to anyone. He is an avid golfer and likes practically any food in the book. He likes to take a nap on the afternoon of a night game. He likes putting on his Cardinal uniform every day during the baseball season.

But there really isn't anything in the world he cares for as much as playing ball with the younger generation. He doesn't have to be urged to take part by any publicity man or image maker. It's simply that he likes to do it, he likes being with the kids, and likes feeling that he can help to steer boys in the right direction.

In recent years two stories that prove beyond a shadow of a doubt the exact qualities of mind and heart than Stan possesses have gained wide circulation.

One is a story told by the novelist Jerome Weidman

in *Sports Illustrated* magazine. It is worth repeating here.

For several days it had rained at St. Petersburg Beach, in Florida, back in the spring of 1955, and Jerome Weidman's two little boys, seven and eight years old, became as restless as caged lions.

Though the skies were still rather leaden, the rains finally stopped and the boys wanted to go out on the beach to throw the ball around. With a borrowed bat and ball the three Weidmans proceeded to the beach. For a while Weidman threw the ball up himself and hit it — and the two boys ran their legs off chasing it. Then, as is always the case when a ball is being batted around, other youngsters were attracted to the scene.

"Can we play, too?" they asked. And Weidman said sure, he'd be delighted to have them.

Now there were six lively boys tearing through the sand after Jerry Weidman's fungoes, and the usually sedentary writer was having himself a grand time. He didn't have to move around much in hitting the ball and he had half a dozen healthy kids to return the ball to him.

Finally, as it must to all good things, an end came to Weidman's picnic: the boys insisted on taking a turn at bat, too. That meant he'd have to do some chasing around in the field. So he relinquished his hold on the bat and ran about 40 or 50 feet down the beach, where he was hopeful the ball would be hit.

Little fellows like this — all of them were below ten years old — don't have much professional skill or power, of course, and in no time at all Weidman discovered that he was wearing himself out chasing balls that were hit just a few feet away into the chilly surf. Each time the ball dribbled into the water he ran after it. Then he'd throw it back to the tiny batter and return to his position in the "outfield," hopeful that the youngster could hit the ball straight at him.

When one of Weidman's boys actually hit one directly at him, he was in for the embarrassment of his life. The ball scooted mischievously between his awkwardly spread legs. With a grunt Weidman straightened up. The prospect of chasing the ball down the beach didn't appeal to his practical sense.

However, lo and behold, before he could turn around and give chase to the ball, the ball came bouncing back toward his heavy-hitting son.

In a second Weidman realized what had happened, as a nice-looking man, properly protected from the cold in a big, blue sweater, came walking by him.

"Awful day," said the man in the blue sweater.

"Yeah," said Weidman, self-conscious about the error he had just made in the field.

Then, while Weidman's eye was still trained on the passer-by, his son threw the ball up and for the second time in a row connected solidly. This time the ball came directly at Weidman. But before it could reach the novelist's outstretched hands the man in the blue sweater stuck out his hand and speared the ball, as nonchalantly as you please.

"What a catch!" the children yelled, gleefully.

The lithe figure in blue grinned somewhat apologetically at Weidman.

"I'm sorry," he said. "But it was coming right at me."

"That's okay," grunted Weidman.

The youngsters continued to cheer the stranger as he walked towards them. Then he noticed one of the boys taking a few practice swings with the bat.

"You know," he began, "I don't think you're holding that bat quite right. Here, mind if I show you?"

The boy — Jerry Weidman's son — handed the man the bat. The other youngsters immediately crowded around, hopeful that they would discover some new secrets from this obliging man. Weidman poked at the sand for a moment with his right foot, then condescended to move towards the spot where the man was holding his free seminar.

"You're pulling the bat too far back over your shoulder," the man said in a quiet voice to Jerry's boy. "When you do that your swing has to travel much too far to connect with the ball. If the pitcher throws his fast ball at you, by the time you get your bat around on it you're probably going to miss it by a mile."

Weidman started to object to the stranger's instruction. After all, the stranger was tearing down the very stance he had taught his son to use. But his instinct told him to be quiet and listen to what the man was telling the kids.

"Try doing it this way," continued the stranger.

He bent over, holding the bat in a left-hander's position. Then he held the bat up straight in front of him, spreading his legs about a foot apart and wiggling his torso just a little, as he demonstrated to his rapt audience.

"Now you're all set for it," he said, swinging the bat on a level line once or twice. "When the pitcher throws it at you, you take your cut and — wham — it's out of the old ball park!"

"Here, you try it now," said the stranger, handing the bat back to Weidman's boy.

Weidman stepped towards the boy. "Just a second," he began. But the stranger interrupted him.

"I'm really very sorry," he said to Weidman. "I didn't mean to take over this thing. Maybe you'd better show the boys a thing or two."

Weidman looked at the boys. Then he peered intently at the stranger in the blue sweater.

"No," he said slowly. "You were doing fine. Keep going."

So the batting seminar on that overcast day in spring continued, under the supervision of the man in blue.

The next day the sun was shining again. When Jerry Weidman arrived on the beach his boys and a dozen others stood in a circle around a man who had his head slightly bent and seemed to be writing something in a little book he held in his hands.

As Weidman came closer to the group, he realized it was the same man who had given his boys batting lessons the previous day. Except the man was now in swimming trunks instead of the blue sweater. As Weidman hit the outer fringe of the group, the man suddenly looked up at him, smiled warmly and nodded. Then his head went down again and he continued to write in the book he held in his hand. When he finished writing he handed the book to Jeff, Weidman's son. And the boy came running over to his father, waving the book aloft in his hand.

"Look, Dad," he said, with triumph in his voice. "Look!"

Weidman took the book — an autograph book — from his boy. With great curiosity he scanned the page to which the book was opened.

Then he read the message that had been scrawled in black ink:

"To Jeff, with the best wishes of Stan Musial."

"That's when everything became all right," concluded Jerome Weidman, in his description of the touching incident.

On another occasion, Stan played a role in a melodramatic situation that ordinarily would rate an incredulous snicker — if it involved anyone but himself. There are an increasing number of tales that are disseminated about athletes and movie performers to establish them as heroes meriting the worship of the multitudes. Many of these tales are figments of a press agent's imagination or are, purely and simply, "put-up jobs." It is commonplace, for instance, for ballyhoo artists of prize fights to arrange for fake "rescues" of someone from a nearby lake during the build-up period before a fight is scheduled to take place. The rescuer, naturally, is one of the principals in the fight. Often, too, "secret" visits to hospitals are arranged to advance the proposition that such-and-such a movie star or ball-player is an individual with a heart of gold.

Stan Musial, however, has never been in need of such fake promotion. He instinctively does the right and decent thing.

In the case of a boy named "Little Joe," who lived in St. Louis, it was Stan's thoughtfulness that helped to restore a youngster to his proper place in the society of other children.

It seems that Little Joe, a boy of eleven years of age, just couldn't get himself to join the daily game of base-ball that was played almost every day after school near the St. Gabriel Church.

Monsignor Leo Steck watched the boy, day after day, as he leaned against a tree. And day after day the boy refused to participate in the choose-up game. He watched the proceedings, silently and sullenly, never making a move to join in the fun.

This, thought Monsignor Steck, is a classic case of a

child devoid of confidence, but with a desperate desire also to belong.

What could be done to get him to play with the others?

One day Monsignor Steck remembered that Stan Musial was a member of his own St. Gabriel Church. He also knew that Stan had a way with youngsters, especially when it came to baseball.

He called Stan and told him about Little Joe.

"I think maybe you can help to get Joe to play with the others," said the Monsignor. "Will you come around tomorrow?"

True to his word, Stan was there the next afternoon. When the boys realized who he was they flocked around him, buzzing and chattering and asking questions.

But Little Joe stayed away from the group.

"Will you play with us, Mr. Musial?" the boys asked.

"Sure," said Stan. "But first I've got to warm up. Lend me two gloves and a ball."

With the gloves and the ball in his hands, Stan ambled over to the little boy next to the tree.

"How would you like to warm me up, son?" said Stan to Little Joe. "A fella my age gets mighty creaky, you know."

Stan chucked the ball underhand to the boy. He caught it. Then Little Joe went over to one of the gloves that Stan had placed on the ground. Picking it up, he examined it carefully, as if it were the rarest of jewels.

"Okay," urged Stan, "throw it here."

Little Joe hesitated a moment, then he took a big windup, the kind he'd seen big-leaguers use on television, and tossed it to Stan.

"That's the way to do it," yelled Stan.

The two of them — Stan, the greatest ballplayer of his time, and Little Joe, the youngster who thought nobody cared — threw the ball back and forth for a few minutes. Each time Little Joe threw his own brand of fast ball, Stan pulled back his gloved hand in a mock gesture of distress.

When the game got under way, Monsignor Steck picked Joe as his first choice. The youngster was asked to play center field. As he trotted out to the position, he smiled shyly for the first time in anyone's memory.

By the seventh inning Monsignor Steck's team was ahead of Stan's team by a run. After two batters were retired on Stan's team the next two walked. This brought the Monsignor running to the mound.

"I think we need a new pitcher, son," said the Monsignor to his pitcher. "I'm going to ask Little Joe to pitch now." So saying he waved to the boy, who was standing in center field.

Little Joe came trotting in. Without saying a word he took his warm-up pitches with his catcher. But when he began to work on the next batter he was wild. The boy walked, loading the bases.

And who should be coming up next? Mr. Musial himself!

While the youngsters held their breaths to see exactly how Mr. Musial would break up the old ball game, Little Joe prepared to work on the hitter.

His first pitch came in nicely and Stan lashed at it and sent it whistling far into right field — foul only by inches. Then Little Joe missed with one, for a ball. On the third pitch Little Joe almost threw the ball away, but the catcher made a nice save.

Little Joe rubbed the ball vigorously in his hand. Then he glared at Mr. Musial. Then he let go. The ball shot down the left-field line, as if it had been bashed out of a cannon. But again it was foul all the way. Stan had swung just a bit too late.

With the count two and two, Little Joe decided to put everything he had on the next pitch. Taking a full windup and rearing back as if he could have been Rapid Robert Feller, Little Joe let loose. The ball whizzed right over the outside corner of the plate that Stan was guarding so jealously. Breaking his famous crouch, Stan went for the ball. But, alas, like Mighty Casey of the famous poem, he struck out!

Within a matter of seconds all of Little Joe's teammates gathered around him on the mound. They pounded him on the back and told him how great he'd been.

"Boy, you struck out Stan Musial," they chirped. "That's something!"

Little Joe smiled and laughed and hit his teammates on the back.

Later, when the tumult subsided, and Monsignor

153

Steck had a chance to speak to Stan privately, the priest said:

"Stan, I think the boy is going to be fine from now on, thanks to you. But let me tell you that you almost gave me heart failure on those two foul balls."

Stan laughed heartily. "I was wondering when you were going to put Joe in to pitch," he said. "But it was pretty enticing to come up there with the bases loaded. I almost forgot myself. It would have broken Joe's heart if I had hit one."

But Stan is not a man who breaks the hearts of children. He'd rather make them smile and laugh — usually along with him.

CHAPTER FOURTEEN

DURABLE STAN

One day in the summer of 1962 Mickey Charles Mantle, plagued as always by an assortment of injuries, said somewhat sadly, as he sat in the Yankee dressing room:

"How old is that fellow Musial? Forty-one? Well, I'd like to change bodies with him — and I'm thirty-one."

Mickey, whose career has been sorely hampered by illnesses and a protesting body, is not the first person to pay tribute to Stan's durability.

If most baseball observers are aware of Stan's innumerable records, many have, nevertheless, overlooked one aspect of his career. That is his capacity to stay in

the Cardinal lineup, day in and day out, over more
than two decades. He is one of the most durable men
ever to have played the game. From April 15, 1952,
through August 22, 1957, Stan ran a consecutive game
streak of 895 games. That meant he appeared in the
St. Louis lineup every day, either in the outfield or at
first base. This is a National League record, breaking
the mark of 822 straight games once held by Pittsburgh's first baseman Gus Suhr. In an era of specialists,
two-platooning, exhausting schedules and increased
night ball, this record may stand for all time.

In the first 16 years of his career, Stan missed only
16 games because of injuries. Only one other player in
major league history, Iron Man Lou Gehrig of the
Yankees, had ever demonstrated such endurance and
spirit on the field of battle. Gehrig's consecutive game
mark of 2,130 contests, of course, is unmatched.

Strangely, though he is seemingly as durable as a Will
Rogers pun and a Late Show movie, Stan doesn't look
the part at all. He is just six feet tall, weighs about 180
most of the time, when he isn't indulging in pastries late
at night, and is somewhat round-shouldered. He is not
the possessor of bulging muscles and does not lift weights
or run barefooted in the forests to keep in shape. He is
simply a fortunate fellow who with few exceptions
over the years has not been pinned down by broken
bones, a rebelling stomach or creeping arthritis.

In the last few seasons, when Stan has been playing
fine ball, to the consternation of the gloom merchants

who can't comprehend what keeps a man going when he is in the late thirties and early forties, Musial has engaged in a vigorous training regimen.

"I've been concentrating on keeping in shape," says Stan. "At the recommendation of the Cards' trainer, Bob Bauman, I've gone to some pains — and I do mean pains —to get myself in top condition through a special six-week exercise program conducted by Dr. Walter Eberhardt of St. Louis University. This helps me feel good for the start of each season. It helps me keep my quick reflexes and meet those fast balls."

In these past few years, of course, Stan has not been making a total effort to play every day, as he did when he was a younger man. His Cardinal managers have rested him frequently, letting him sit out the second games of twin bills and those afternoon games that have followed night games. However, there was a time when Stan rebelled when he wasn't used every day.

During the long consecutive game streak, Stan paid little or no attention to minor injuries. He was the original man "who came to play." Once, in 1956, when he hurt his wrist, he insisted on prolonging the streak by making token appearances in the St. Louis lineup until the injury healed. However, this policy did not win widespread praise. There were those who felt the record really wasn't being preserved in the proper way — and Stan later acknowledged that he had made something of a mistake in judgment.

"I'd never do that again," he said. "It took too much

out of me, getting in there every day. I think if I'd have taken a day off every now and then it would have done far more for me and I'd have stayed stronger for a longer time."

The 895-game string ended abruptly one day late in August, when the Cards were in Philadelphia, facing fast-baller Jack Sanford. At the time Stan was in a hot streak at the plate and the Cards were giving the Milwaukee Braves a run for the National League flag.

With Wally Moon on first base, Manager Fred Hutchinson signaled for a hit-and-run play. Trying to protect his base runner, and also hit behind him, if possible, Stan swung viciously at a pitch that was far and away. When he did, something went plop in his left shoulder. It turned out that he had yanked his left arm out of its socket, fractured a bone of the shoulder socket and torn the muscles over the collarbone and shoulder blade.

It was a rough break for the Cards, literally and figuratively, for the injury sent Stan to the bench for three weeks, during which time he missed 20 ball games. Meanwhile the Cards continued to chase the Braves for the pennant, minus their biggest gun.

Stan wanted so much to get back into the lineup that he kept telling Hutchinson he was ready when he actually wasn't. Even when Fred finally gave in and let Stan pinch-hit, Musial could hardly lift his arm.

However, Stan wanted to be in the regular starting

array, so he asked Hutchinson to watch how many tough chances came the way of his successor at first base.

"Heck, Hutch," reasoned Stan, "he hasn't had a really hard one in a week. I could take care of that job even with one arm."

The argument won the day for Musial, and he returned to the Card lineup, to help in the last-ditch fight for the pennant.

As things turned out Stan went on another of his famous hitting sprees, batting over .350 after he went back to first base. The flood of base hits earned him his seventh batting title, and probably his last, unless he wins one when he's forty-two or forty-three years old. But the Cards lost out to the Braves in the final week of the season, much to Stan's chagrin.

"I wanted that pennant more than the batting title," he said.

It is interesting to note that if Stan hadn't taken a day off, with some reservations, on the last day of the 1951 season, his long string of consecutive games would have gone well over 1,000.

Stan wanted to play that day, as always. But Manager Marty "Slats" Marion, once the fancy-fielding shortstop of the Cards, insisted that his buddy should sit it out.

"You deserve a rest, Stan," Marion said. "Why not sit down today? The season is over."

Even when he wasn't feeling in his usual robust state of health, Musial rarely ever asked for any special consideration or treatment from his manager. He has never been the kind of athlete who pampers himself or tries to favor himself when he is under the weather.

There was the time, some years ago, that Stan arrived at Ebbets Field in Brooklyn, his old happy hunting ground, and the prospect of banging a few doubles off those inviting walls overrode the fact that he wasn't feeling well. So he played as usual that day, refusing to beg off from active duty.

However, during the course of the game, Stan was extremely active in the field. On one of his catches he robbed a perplexed Dodger with a stab that sent him reeling on his shoulder. This was the same member that had kicked up when he was a kid ballplayer and had forced his change from pitcher to outfielder. Stan didn't tip off his manager about it when the shoulder started to pain him, but in the last half of the ninth inning, when Brooklyn staged a rally, he came jogging in from the outfield.

Manager Eddie Dyer came to the front of the dugout to find out what was on Stan's mind.

"I think you'd better take me out, Skip," said Stan.

"Why?" asked Dyer, who could never recall Stan making a demand like this in the past.

"I hurt my shoulder making that catch earlier in the game," said Stan, "and if Pete [Reiser was the next

160

Dodger batter] hits one to me I may not be able to throw to the plate to head a run off."

"Okay, we'll put Diering in," said Dyer.

Despite his indestructibility, Stan has been haunted frequently by the specter of serious injury.

When he went into the restaurant business in St. Louis with Biggie Garagnani, Musial did it primarily for financial security.

"I figured I ought to have something to fall back on," he said. "You never know what's going to happen to you in this game. One bad injury and you can be through for life, or just a season."

Stan, of course, has had his share of emergencies, too. One was the battle with his appendix in 1947. Another was when he slipped in a game at Pittsburgh's Forbes Field in 1950 and wound up walking around like a hobbled horse.

"I thought it was worse than it really was," recalls Stan. "When I first tried to get up on my feet, I couldn't. When I fell back I had the notion this was the end for me. But it turned out to be nothing."

Nevertheless, Stan had to wear an elastic band to support the knee. And he didn't remove it for some time.

Trainer Bob Bauman of the Cards, who has seen hundreds of athletes on his rubbing table, is one of Stan's perpetual admirers.

"He's in a class by himself. He can stand pain that would make most men fold up. I've never heard him complain in all the years I've known him," says Bauman.

Bauman can remember any number of trying occasions for Musial. But one in particular stands out in his memory.

In 1957 Stan had a four-for-four day, as he opened the season against the Reds. But in the course of having his perfect first day at the plate, Stan suffered a painful back injury. "The muscles were in spasm, bunched up as hard as ridged wood," wrote St. Louis sportswriter Bob Broeg. And it appeared that Stan was due for a long period of recuperation.

However, that's not the way Stan looked at the problem. He wanted to play badly, coming off an inferior — for him — 1956 season, when he hit "only" .310.

"I want to get back in there right away," he told Bauman.

So the Card trainer sprayed Stan's troublesome back muscle with a stream of freezing ethyl chloride, hoping to relax the area. Then he bundled Stan The Man in bandages and waited to see what would happen. What happened was that Stan was in the lineup the next time the Cards played.

"He's got the body of a seventeen-year-old," says Bauman, who never ceases to wonder at his prize patient. "His body is supple as a kid's. I've never seen anything like it."

CHAPTER FIFTEEN

THE AMAZING 1962 SEASON

The year of 1959 was the one that Stan Musial would like best to forget. "That was the worst season of my career," acknowledges Stan. It was, too.

Stan hit 80 or 100 points below his accustomed level. (His final average was .255 on 87 hits.) "Sportswriters and friends wondered out loud whether I shouldn't quit for good," says Stan.

Well, Stan *didn't quit*. He added up all the pros and cons, all the pluses and minuses, and decided to keep going.

"I don't know when I'm going to retire from this game," said Stan. "But I've given a lot of thought to the

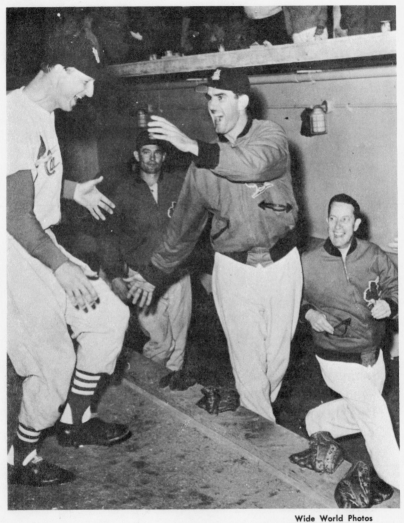

In 1962, Stan Musial batted .330 and brought his lifetime total of hits to a National League record. Here he is greeted in the dugout when his 3,431st hit eclipsed the old record posted by Honus Wagner.

matter these last few years, and before I ever make a decision I've got to consider three things:

"One. If I still get a thrill out of the game.

"Two. If I'm still proud of my batting average, my RBI's and my throwing arm.

"Three. And most important of all — if I still feel I can genuinely help the team.

"When I lose any one of these three incentives, I'm going to call it a day, no matter how much it hurts. Until then, I'm not quitting!"

There was no doubt, however, that 1959 almost retired Stan to private life. It was as close as he has come, since 1941, to getting out of baseball.

This was the summer when Musial, one of the handful of men in history to stroke over 3,000 hits, was told by Manager Solly Hemus, a man with a tissue-weight lifetime batting average, that he could no longer hit curve balls the way a big-leaguer should. It was the summer when an accumulation of 17 baseball years and uncounted aches, pains and wounds of ball games long forgotten, finally took an inevitable toll on Stan The Man. It was the summer when the baseball writers began to warm up shiny obituaries for Stan. It was the summer when Stan, a man with a collection of bowling alleys, banks and restaurants, suddenly became too old to play baseball — the way Stan Musial should.

In 1959 Stan also discovered that if he was going to continue to play and to pursue Honus Wagner's National League mark for total hits, he was going to have to do it without the benefit of the leg hits, the bleeders, the bunts. He was going to have to carry on without the reflexes that had once served him so well.

"My reflexes just don't bounce back now," admitted Stan.

So Stan Musial was in the Cardinal lineup again in 1960 and 1961. And though it was obvious he was not the Musial of 10 years earlier, he still tried hard and had a continual affection for the ringing sound of a base hit off his bat. Driven by the quiet pride of an outstanding professional, Stan batted .275 in 1960 and went up to .288 in 1961. Courageously, now that he was in the sunset of his career, he was beginning to work his way up in the averages again.

Arthur Daley, the sports columnist of *The New York Times,* wrote, in March 1962, as Stan prepared for his 21st active season in a St. Louis uniform:

"Whatever the years have done to Stan Musial, they have not dimmed his boyish enthusiasm . . . he is as sprightly and eager for the start of another season, as he was for his first full season in 1942."

In St. Petersburg, Florida, Stan told the reporters that he would keep playing as long as it was fun for him. And, by golly, it still seemed to be fun — and he still seemed to be a help to the Cards.

"I don't want to become the oldest man ever to play big league ball," he said. "But I checked the records and both Ty Cobb and Honus Wagner were still at it when they were forty-three or so. And I'm just a kid of forty-one!"

Chronological age, of course, is never the true barometer of a man's desires or abilities or worth, unless the man himself is burdened and saddled by the weight of his own years. We have only to look around us and see a clear-cut demonstration of this in the lives and experiences of such public figures as Herbert Hoover, at·eighty-eight; Bernard Baruch, at ninety-two; Winston Churchill and Konrad Adenauer, both in their eighties; and the proud Charles DeGaulle, in his seventies. In sports, we don't have to look any further than that jolly and voluble personality Casey Stengel, and others like ancient Archie Moore and the pitching perennial Satchel Paige.

A New York rabbi, Sanford Seltzer, who may have had any of these durable and distinguished gentlemen in mind, said in a radio broadcast over CBS, in August 1962:

"A major league baseball player is considered old and washed up at thirty-five. A United States Senator is thought rather young at the same age. . . . Let us always remember that one is as young as his faith, as old as his doubts, as young as his confidence, as old as his fears, as young as his hope, as old as his despair."

The faith of Stan Musial in himself was still unbounded, even when he approached the proposition of

167

facing National League pitching at the ripe old age of forty-one.

He still had a buoyancy of spirit, a determination and a sense of pride that enabled him to blithely ignore the lengthening shadows of time.

When asked repeatedly why he didn't hang up his spikes, Stan would only grin — that boyish grin that had always captivated the writers and the fans — and try to explain his motivation in continuing.

"I don't want to sound corny," he'd say, "but baseball has been so much a part of my life for so long that I'd miss it terribly. I never imagined it would be so hard to quit. Year after year it's always been the same. I feel no older and I can't wait to start spring training."

For many players the routine of spring training is drudgery, a time of sore muscles and the monotonous grind of exhibition games. Many often feel the same way about the regular season schedule, now an almost interminable 162 games.

But to Stan Musial baseball is all. Joe Williams of the New York *World Telegram & Sun* wrote in 1962 that "you'd have to see Stan in spring training, where the formalities are less restrictive than in league competition, to appreciate the zest he has for the sport. If he isn't swinging a bat, he's playing catch ball. If he isn't running in the outfield, he's shagging flies. A stranger would take him for a rookie, striving to catch the manager's attention. To Musial the work was pleasure."

But Stan was no unrealistic Pollyanna. He knew that at his age he had to operate under certain handicaps. He knew he'd need more rest, more time off. But when he acknowledged these things to himself, along with the other limitations, he still felt he had one considerable advantage working for him. That was his batting eye.

One day, about a year ago, he was sitting around in a restaurant having a friendly chat with several writers. Ed Linn, a magazine journalist, asked him what he thought of his chances of having another .300 batting year. Linn was referring to the fact that in 1959, 1960 and 1961 he had failed to reach that level, which used to be easy as apple pie for him.

Suddenly the expression on Stan's face hardened. He leaned forward slightly in his chair, and looked directly into Linn's eyes.

"Ed, maybe I can't field much any more," he said. "And maybe I can't run much. But let me tell you, I can still hit!"

Despite this unalterable confidence in his batting prowess, Stan could never have dreamed that 1962 would wind up for him as a page out of the 1940s, when he functioned as the most prolific hitter in his league.

If anyone had whispered to Stan before the start of the season that he would actually lead the National League in hitting for a good part of the year and battle

Tommy Davis of the Los Angeles Dodgers and Frank Robinson of the Cincinnati Reds for the batting title over the last part of the season, he would have chuckled in his inimitable way and have said:

"Mister, you're nuts!"

But that is exactly what happened.

If anyone had predicted that in the last week of the season, when the Dodgers and the Giants groggily fought each other down to the wire for the elusive pennant, Stan would hit Giant pitching for five-for-five in one important game, and deliver the key hits in the other crucial games against the Dodgers, a psychiatrist might have been in order for the predictor.

But, again, that *is* what happened.

It was that kind of a season for Stan, forty-one years young.

Dan Parker said it better than anybody else one day in his New York *Mirror* column.

"In view of the monotony of listing Stan's record-setting achievements, which now occur almost every time he comes to bat, wouldn't it be more in order (with no disrespect intended The Man) to treat as unusual only those days on which Stan doesn't do anything unusual?"

On April 12, 1962, a near-freezing day in St. Louis, Stan served notice on all concerned that he'd been slumbering a bit the past few years and that he had been gulping greedily from the Fountain of Youth.

As the Cards walloped the New York Mets, 11–4, Stan had a perfect three-for-three day at the plate, with two singles and the good old Musial two-base hit. He drove in two runs and carried in another himself.

When he scored his run, the statisticians, who were in a state of exhaustion all season trying to keep up with Stan's never-ending record-shattering, were quick to point out that this tied him with Mel Ott, at 1,859 runs, for the National League record. It didn't take long for that record to go, either. For the next afternoon, Stan did it.

"Stan came roaring out the starting gate for 1962," editorialized *The Sporting News,* baseball's revered weekly, which has never ceased to applaud his achievements. "He thoroughly enjoys playing the game at forty-one as much as he did at twenty-one. This, by many miles, is Musial's greatest asset."

Stan's run-scoring record served to point up his skill as a base runner. It is a talent that he has always had, but which, under his avalanche of base hits, has generally gone unnoticed and unpraised. Not that he is a Maury Wills or a Ty Cobb on the bases. He is not. However, he has always been a skillful base runner, with uncanny judgment, an ability to take the extra base, and the instinct and reflexes of a race car driver.

Despite the fact that Musial has rarely been followed in the Card lineup by great sluggers, he has managed to score 100 or more runs 11 times, for a National League mark. His finesse and polish in running the bases contributed more to his success in this department than any of the men who batted behind him in the Card battle array.

Just to prove his abilities in the department of base-running, Stan stole second base against the Chicago Cubs in the third game of the 1962 season. It was only his second stolen base in five seasons, but it put the Cubs and the rest of the league on notice that that old man Musial would bear watching — even when he dropped his bat and trotted down to first base. Stan also hit a home run in the same game. But it was the theft of second that drew smiles from Dick Musial, Stan's son, who came out to Wrigley Field to see his dad play.

"You know, my boy Dick came over from Notre Dame to watch us play the Cubs," said Stan, "and he got a much bigger kick out of watching me steal second than he did in seeing me hit my home run with a man on base."

In those early days of the season, most of the Midwest cities that Stan traveled to were beset by icy weather and skin-splitting winds. That included his home bailiwick of St. Louis. Manager Johnny Keane of the Cards, cooperating in the effort to conserve Stan's energy and protect him against the elements, was quite concerned about whether or not he should play Musial under such precarious conditions.

172

"I'd go over to Stan and ask him about it," said Keane, "and he'd always insist 'I'm fine, don't worry about me,' so I just stopped wasting my time asking him."

It was clear that despite his status as his team's elder statesman Stan wanted no special favors.

As April's harsh weather faded into the more balmy days of May and June, Stan found himself having not only a good year at bat, but a spectacular one. At the end of April, playing before an appreciative Sunday home town crowd, Stan went all the way in both games of a double-header against the Reds, made five hits in six times at bat, scored four runs, and drove in two. This was the man who was supposed to be fading away. At the least, this was the player who was not expected to be playing through any tiring twin bills.

With things rolling along so well for him, Stan, who usually shrugged off records that he was piling up as just part of his daily work, now looked forward with keen anticipation to smashing one particular record: Honus Wagner's all-time National League mark for hits, 3,430.

One day, when he knew he had only 18 hits to go to tie Honus, and 19 to beat him, Stan said: "Well, you've got to give these kids something to shoot for, don't you?"

Wagner, the Hall of Fame Pirate shortstop, was coming in for his full share of Stan's attention. On May 5,

173

when Stan made two hits and scored two runs against Cincinnati, he also tied Wagner's record for most games played in the National League.

The next day, once again playing through both games of a double-header, Stan smashed Wagner's mark, when he participated in his 2,786th game. Just to add a more memorable touch to the affair Stan came up in the ninth inning of the scoreless second game and knocked Moe Drabowski's (remember him?) pitch into the right-field bleachers, with two men on base, to win the game for Bob Gibson, 3–0.

Someone, the following day, risked toting up the number of National League records that Stan held. The figure was established at 39. But it was the 40th record that Stan was now bearing down on. And that was the one that he really wanted more than all the others. Certainly this was what he wanted more than anything since the 3,000th hit.

CHAPTER SIXTEEN

THE BIGGEST HIT

As Stan fought his way to tie and then pass Honus Wagner's National League record for total hits — which the knock-kneed Pittsburgh great had set back in 1917, some 45 years before — he began to experience the kind of persistent pressure that rookies often feel in their first World Series.

Stan's teammates knew, too, that he was working under intense pressure to pass Wagner. All they had to do was take a long, hard look at the batting averages through the days of May 10 through May 15. On the morning of May 10, Stan, enjoying a fantastic early-season spree, was hitting .394. On the morning of May 15, he was down some 80 points from that level. He had gone to bat 15 times in an effort to land his record-tying hit and had walked away each time, frustrated and slightly bewildered at his ineptitude.

"I never worked for a hit harder in my life," said Stan.

In an effort to lighten Stan's load as much as possible his teammates needled and prodded him, but ever so understandingly. They wanted that hit — or those two hits — almost as much as The Man did.

Only a few days before Stan was to pass Wagner's mark, Bill White, the Card first baseman, kidded him gently in the Card dressing room.

"Hey, Stan, how come they gave you a certificate as a graduate of American Legion baseball?" said Bill. "Red [Schoendienst] says there couldn't have been a Legion when you were that age because they hadn't fought the war yet."

Stan, who likes to kid and to be kidded in turn, laughed happily at the remark. He could stand a little humor in his life at this stage of the game, as he went out again in search of his private Holy Grail.

The fact that practically everybody who had any interest in baseball was rooting for him to accomplish his mission, didn't make things easier. In San Francisco, where they took defeat bitterly and gloomily, until that ecstatic and improbable moment of victory in the thrilling 1962 playoff against the Dodgers, the fans begged Stan to make his 3,430th hit. One night, with Billy

O'Dell pitching for the Giants, Stan looked pitiful on four straight trips to the plate — and the fans moaned and groaned each time Stan failed. Even Warren Giles, the National League president, who had flown in from Cincinnati to be on hand for what he hoped would be the historic moment, was disturbed by Stan's frustrations.

"This is a big thing to me," said Giles. "I had to fly over as soon as I was sure the weather was OK."

After the game Stan attempted to be philosophical about his failure of the moment. "It might take me a week, maybe more, to make that hit, because I want it so much," he said. "It's like the time many years ago in Pittsburgh when my mother came to see me play for the first time as a big-leaguer. I played through both games of a double-header and couldn't come up with anything that even looked like a hit."

At long last, after fretting and fuming through several games of fruitless hit-chasing, Stan faced Juan Marichal, the high-kicking, stylish right-hander of the San Francisco Giants, on the afternoon of May 16, at the Giants' Candlestick Park.

In the sixth inning, when Ernie Broglio of the Cards was ahead, in a 1–0 ball game, Stan went over to the rack to pick out his weapon of assault to face Marichal.

Broglio grabbed Stan's uniform, alongside of the left arm. "I got a feeling about this one," said Ernie. "This is gonna be the hit."

For a few seconds Broglio rubbed Stan's arm playfully.

"I hope you're right," said Stan, as he grinned back at Ernie. Then he put on his batting helmet and moved out to the on-deck circle, where he could mull over his approach to the subject by himself.

In a matter of minutes Broglio's hunch was proven right. Swinging at the third pitch served up to him by Marichal, Stan sent the 3,430th hit of his career hopping and skipping into right-center field. In the ninth, when Marichal walked Stan on four pitches, the crowd booed. They wanted the record breaker to follow on the same afternoon. The old equalizer had come hard for Stan, and he was the first to admit it in the dressing room after the game, which, incidentally, the Cards ended up losing, 7–2.

"I had a terrible time getting up for this hit," said Stan. "Maybe I can get up for the breaking one."

Now it remained for Stan to visit the other West Coast ball park, Chavez Ravine, the home of the Los Angeles Dodgers, to continue the pursuit of the single hit that would etch his name into the record for all time as the most prolific hitter in his league's history.

On a Saturday night in Los Angeles, over 50,000 partisan Dodger fans came out to root Musial home to his destiny, a highly unlikely situation in a town noted for its local loyalties.

Stan, the true dramatist, stretched out the agony and waiting until the ninth inning. Then, facing Dodger relief pitcher Ron Perranoski, Stan lined a good curve into right field, where Frank Howard, a large, lumbering outfielder, snared it on the first bounce and whipped it back to the infield. Wally Moon, the Dodger first baseman, who once played on the Cards with Stan, retrieved the throw from Howard, and examined the ball for a second as if he expected to find "3,431st hit" carved in writing on the face of the horsehide. Then he walked over to Stan, who stood smiling at first base, and handed him the ball.

"Wally was all set to shake my hand," said Stan later, "but he pulled back at the last instant." The rule against fraternization on the ball field still stood up, even at such a moment, and Moon realized it.

Under ordinary circumstances, Manager Keane would have sent in a runner immediately for Stan. But he decided not to do it. "I kept looking for Don Landrum to come out and pick me up at first," said Stan, "because I wanted to get out of there. I just about wilted when I got to first with the record hit."

But Landrum didn't come trotting out to relieve his teammate. "With such a huge crowd on hand, cheering Stan wildly," said the manager, "I wanted to have Stan stay out there as long as possible." When the cheering finally subsided, Landrum replaced Stan at first.

As Stan returned to the Card dugout, he was greeted by a mob scene.

"You got it!" his teammates howled in glee.

"I got, I got it!" Stan chirped back at them.

This was a happy man. No ballplayer could have had a more satisfying moment. Not even Roger Maris, when he poled home run number 61, on the last day of the 1961 season.

Stan had only two slight disappointments connected with his record-breaking effort. One was that his loyal comrade at home, his wife Lil, hadn't been on hand to share the occasion with him, as she had been on hand so many other times. She was back home in St. Louis and had fully intended to take in the proceedings by radio. But, feeling tired and tense, she had fallen off to sleep before the game came on late at night from the West Coast.

"I missed the whole thing on radio," she said sadly, "and by the time I woke up Stan had done his work for the evening."

Then she thought for a moment about why she had fallen asleep. "I guess I'm just too old for this game," she said. "It's only for young people like Stan."

Stan's other minor disappointment was that he hadn't been able to connect for his record-breaking poke before a home town audience. It was the same story as the 3,000th hit off Moe Drabowsky — when he did it before a Chicago crowd.

"I guess I should be happy with the fact that I did it, anyway, in a beautiful new park and against the Dodgers," said Stan.

As for Ron Perranoski, who threw the ball that put Stan over the hump in his chase after Wagner's mark, he wasn't too concerned about his role in making history this way.

"There were a lot of other pitchers he hit," said Ron, "to get up to where he did. I threw him a good curve ball and he hit it. I'm glad he hit it when he did instead of a week earlier in St. Louis when it might have cost us a ball game."

Under ordinary circumstances, and if Stan Musial has been an ordinary fellow, this hit against Perranoski would have been the true climax of an incredible career. At least it would have climaxed the season for Stan. But, as that perennial wit Joe Garagiola keeps reminding everyone, Stan is no ordinary fellow.

"He's a saint with money," cracked Joe, an ex-teammate of Stan's, who now gets paid for being funny on television and radio, while broadcasting baseball games.

The "saint with money" had no intention of curtailing his hit production, simply because he was the new all-time champ of his league.

A few days after he made his 3,341st hit, Monmouth College, in Monmouth, Illinois, honored The Man by presenting him with an Honorary Doctor of Humanities degree. The National League pitchers, who have never felt that Stan has shown any special humane consideration for their health, must have been shocked by Monmouth's award. But nobody else was.

Following the award Stan went about his daily chores as usual. Except, in the season of 1962, there was really nothing usual about it. After all, this was an aged warrior, this man Musial. At the age of forty-one he had survived long past the common career span of ballplayers.

Men who had once played, and shared headline space with him, men who could be truly considered his contemporaries, had long since given up the game. There was Ted Williams, now plugging away for a sporting goods company, and Joe DiMaggio, more in the news as an ex-husband of the ill-fated Marilyn Monroe than as a ballplayer of renown. There was Hank Greenberg, involved in front office business. And Enos Slaughter, the once imperishable commodity, who had finally stopped running. And Jackie Robinson, who was involved with a restaurant chain and civil rights matters.

These and others had come and gone. But Stan still kept going, still kept hitting, still kept trying.

His reflexes still seemed as sharp as ever in this remarkable year of 1962 and his muscles still seemed resilient and rubbery. His ambitions in baseball, and for baseball, still seemed limitless and his spirit was undaunted. He still played the game he loved more than anything else in the world like a young boy on a grimy sandlot.

"Even now," said Leo Durocher, "there is still only one way to pitch to this guy — under the plate."

Here he was, a man attending graduation ceremonies for his daughter Geraldine, from the Villa Duchesne School in St. Louis, and for his son Dick, from Notre Dame, and yet he was possessed of the same spirit and desire as his own youngsters.

"That's another record for the book," joked Joe Garagiola, when he heard that Stan had made both graduations and had also picked up the degree from Monmouth College, all within a few days. "Most graduations in one week, three by Stan Musial."

But Stan wasn't confining his activities to formal educational ceremonies. He was still busting that ball, good and proper. One day it was a game-winning homer in the 11th inning against the Cincinnati Reds; the next it was three hits, including a homer, against the Philadelphia Phillies, that helped him shatter Ty Cobb's all-time record for total bases; the next a three-run homer to beat the Chicago Cubs, 8–6; the next three homers to wallop the New York Mets.

"We usually don't like to play him more than a week at a stretch," said Manager Johnny Keane, whose eyes were popping at Stan's performance. "Then we like to give him a few days of rest. But he's a marvel with that level, steady stroke at bat. I've never seen anything like him!"

One day he posed for a picture with Diomedes Olivo, an aged relief pitcher for the Pittsburgh Pirates (now with the Cards), and probably one of the oldest rookies ever to hit the majors. Diomedes explained, in his best broken English, that Stan had always been his baseball idol.

Looking over at Stan happily, Diomedes said:

"Hundred years, we two."

Stan put on a fake scowl. "What do you mean a hundred years?" he said. "That'd mean you better be fifty-nine, mister, 'cuz *all* I am is forty-one."

And that's the way Stan approaches the matter of his age today. *All* he was in 1962 was forty-one, *all* he'll be in 1963 is forty-two, and *all* he'll be in 1964 is forty-three!

At mid-season of 1962, when Stan was picked, as usual, on the National League All-Star squad, an old friend of his in the White House in Washington, D. C., decided it would be an excellent time to have a reunion.

So the day after the National League licked the American League, 3–1, in the new District of Columbia Stadium (Stan pinch-hit a single in the sixth inning to start a rally that won the ball game), President Kennedy invited Stan over to his residence for a chat. Stan had spoken to the President briefly at the All-Star

Game, and when Stan walked away, the President had said to those in his box: "Wouldn't it be wonderful if the old man got a hit?" Stan then obliged, without even knowing of President Kennedy's wish.

During the game the President outwardly cheered The Man. When Stan's mates on the All-Star squad told him about that, he was terribly proud.

"The President is my buddy," he said, with a big grin. "When I shook hands with him before the game he told the people in his party what a good job of campaigning I did for him in the 1960 election."

But now at the White House Stan was really given a red-carpet treatment. The President presented him with a PT-109 tie pin and an autographed picture. Then he was conducted on a special tour of the White House.

The President, who has always been an enthusiastic sports fan, as well as a passingly good performer in swimming and football, had several questions for Stan. He asked him how many homers he'd hit in his career (the number was 456 up to the time of the All-Star Game) and wanted to know directly from Stan's lips how much longer he thought he would play.

"I just take one game at a time these days," answered Stan. "I hardly ever think about it by the season."

When the excitement of his White House visit was over and Stan had to return to the more humdrum task of terrorizing enemy hurlers again, there wasn't the slightest sign of a letdown in Stan's play.

He found himself in a three-way battle for the National League batting title — his eighth, if he could possibly make it — with Frank Robinson of the Reds and Los Angeles' hot hitter of the year, Tommy Davis. Stan's chances were so good that Johnny Keane began to let him play more and more, instead of less and less. Then, when the hectic National League race came down to the finish, with the Cards having a definite voice in who would represent the National League, San Francisco or Los Angeles, Keane felt that it would be only fair to start Musial in almost every game that his club played against the two main contenders.

One day, when Keane did let Stan sit out one of these crucial ball games, he later felt impelled to call on Stan in the eighth inning for a pinch-hit chore. Stan responded by walloping a three-run homer, his 19th of the year, to narrow San Francisco's margin to 4–3. The Cards dropped the game eventually, 6–3. But Stan had thrown a fright into Giant hopes, for a few moments, with his big blast.

On September 27, with the Giants battling to stay alive in the race for the flag with the Dodgers, the Cards beat the San Franciscans, 7–4. All that Stan did that afternoon was to play left field like a twenty-five-year-old and bang out five straight hits in five trips to the plate!

Only a few months before, Stan had been trying to explain why he would never really be able to hit for a high average again.

186

"You know, these old legs won't be able to give me any more of those big three-for-three or four-for-four days that fatten the old batting average," he said, thoughtfully.

His wonderful show against the straining Giants proved him wrong — but he was delighted to have such bad judgment about his own prowess.

When the Cards then journeyed over to Chavez Ravine for three games — all of which they won, by the way — to finish up the season for the Dodgers, Stan played in each game. Keane, by that time, didn't want to keep The Man on the sidelines and thus subject himself or Stan to the criticism that the Giants might have leveled at him if he had held Stan out.

Though his own team was not fighting for the big prize, Stan was right in there in the thick of it, where he wanted to be. He was an enormous factor in those dying days of a torrid National League struggle and Johnny Keane knew it.

So did Manager Walt Alston of the Dodgers.

In the first of the three final games played at Los Angeles' ball park, Stan made two key hits, as Larry Jackson trimmed the fading Dodgers, 3–2. One of the hits batted in a run early in the game. The other kept a 10th-inning rally going, until the winning run came across.

So, right down to the wire, Stan Musial, forty-one, tired but happy, was playing for keeps. The Giants, ultimate winners of the flag in a delirious and heart-stopping three-game playoff against the Dodgers, would be very pleased not to see him again operating out of that peekaboo crouch. The Dodgers felt the same way, maybe more so.

The only thing Stan Musial was not able to do in 1962 was to hit his team into the World Series. He played in 135 games, 35 more than he ever expected to get into before the start of the season, made 143 hits and batted .330. His final average was the third highest in the National League. As a pinch hitter he went to bat 13 times and connected safely on eight occasions.

One observer, with a keen sense of humor and an even keener appreciation of Stan Musial, cracked, at the season's end, that it would be a fine idea to have Stan voted onto the National League flag winner.

"How can they play a World Series without this fellow?" he said. "He belongs there just once more before he trips over his beard. Why don't the Yanks be nice guys and let him play. He's too good to do without."

If Stan Musial keeps playing long enough for his one and only team, the Cards, he might still get into another World Series.

Don't bet that he won't.

STAN MUSIAL'S
FIRST 21 YEARS

Year	Club	League	Pos.	G.	AB.	R.	H.	HR.	RBI.	B.A.
1938—Williamson	Mt. St.	P	26	62	5	16	1	6	.258
1939—Williamson	Mt. St.	P-PH	23	71	10	25	1	9	.352
1940—Daytona Beach	Fla. St.	OF-P	113	405	55	126	1	70	.311
1941—Springfield	W. A.	OF	87	348	100	132	26	94	.379
1941—Rochester	Int.	OF	54	221	43	72	3	21	.326
1941—St. Louis	Nat.	OF	12	47	8	20	1	7	.426
1942—St. Louis	Nat.	OF	140	467	87	147	10	72	.315
1943—St. Louis	Nat.	OF	157	617	108	220	13	81	.357
1944—St. Louis	Nat.	OF	146	568	112	197	12	94	.347
1945—St. Louis	Nat.				(Military Service)				
1946—St. Louis	Nat.	1B-OF	156	624	124	228	16	103	.365
1947—St. Louis	Nat.	1B	149	587	113	183	19	95	.312
1948—St. Louis	Nat.	OF-1B	155	611	135	230	39	131	.376
1949—St. Louis	Nat.	OF-1B	157	612	128	207	36	123	.338
1950—St. Louis	Nat.	OF-1B	146	555	105	192	28	109	.346
1951—St. Louis	Nat.	OF-1B	152	578	124	205	32	108	.355
1952—St. Louis	Nat.	OF-1B-P	154	578	105	194	21	91	.336
1953—St. Louis	Nat.	OF	157	593	127	200	30	113	.337
1954—St. Louis	Nat.	OF-1B	153	591	120	195	35	126	.330
1955—St. Louis	Nat.	1B-OF	154	562	97	179	33	108	.319
1956—St. Louis	Nat.	1B-OF	156	594	87	184	27	109	.310
1957—St. Louis	Nat.	1B	134	502	82	176	29	102	.351
1958—St. Louis	Nat.	1B	135	472	64	159	17	62	.337
1959—St. Louis	Nat.	1B-OF	115	341	37	87	14	44	.255
1960—St. Louis	Nat.	OF-1B	116	331	49	91	17	63	.275
1961—St. Louis	Nat.	OF	123	372	46	107	15	70	.288
1962—St. Louis	Nat.	OF	135	433	57	143	19	82	.330

WORLD SERIES RECORD

Year	Club	League	Pos.	G.	AB.	R.	H.	HR.	RBI.	B.A.
1942—St. Louis	Nat.	OF	5	18	2	4	0	2	.222
1943—St. Louis	Nat.	OF	5	18	2	5	0	0	.278
1944—St. Louis	Nat.	OF	6	23	2	7	1	2	.304
1946—St. Louis	Nat.	1B	7	27	3	6	0	4	.222

ALL-STAR GAME RECORD

Year	League	Pos.	AB.	R.	H.	HR.	RBI.	B.A.
1943—National		OF	4	0	1	0	1	.250
1944—National		OF	4	1	1	0	1	.250
1946—National		OF	2	0	0	0	0	.000
1947—National		PH	1	0	0	0	0	.000
1948—National		OF	4	1	2	1	2	.500
1949—National		OF	4	1	3	1	2	.750
1950—National		1B	5	0	0	0	0	.000
1951—National		OF	4	1	2	1	1	.500
1952—National		OF	2	1	0	0	0	.000
1953—National		OF	4	0	2	0	0	.500
1954—National		OF	5	1	2	0	0	.400
1955—National		OF	4	1	1	1	1	.250
1956—National		OF	4	1	1	1	1	.250
1957—National		1B	3	1	1	0	0	.333
1958—National		1B	4	1	1	0	0	.250
1959—National		PH-1B	1	0	0	0	0	.000
1960—National		PH	2	1	2	1	1	1.000
1961—National		PH	2	0	0	0	0	.000
1962—National		PH-OF	3	0	1	0	0	.333

189

INDEX

190

The Author

RAY ROBINSON played freshman baseball at Columbia University. He graduated in 1941, served in the U.S. Army, then attended Columbia Law School. Currently articles editor of *Good Housekeeping* magazine, Robinson formerly was managing editor of *Pageant* magazine and senior editor of *Coronet* magazine. He has written sports articles for most of the national magazines. He is also editor of the annual *Baseball Stars* (1958 to 1963) published by Pyramid Books. Robinson lives in Manhattan with his wife and three children, when not in his summer home on Fire Island.